Listen to Me

Beth Huffman

May you enjoy This story about unconditional love.

Beth Huffman

FIRST EDITION

ISBN: 978-1-936989-99-7

Library of Congress Control Number: 2013911667

Published by
NewBookPublishing.com, a division of Reliance Media, Inc.
515 Cooper Commerce Drive, #140, Apopka, FL 32703
NewBookPublishing.com

Printed in the United States of America

Dedication

*T*his book is dedicated to my husband, Herb, whose love and loyalty sustain me always. I could never live this dream of being an author and inspirational speaker without him.

This book is also dedicated in memory of my parents, Helen and Richard Needler, who never discouraged my free-spirited ventures. While other young girls wanted a doll or a kite in their Easter baskets, I hoped for colored pencils and a pad of yellow paper to write stories with happy endings. The Easter Bunny and my parents never let me down. Neither has Herb.

Acknowledgements

I enjoyed and respected Kim Brinkman when she was my student in middle school. Little did I know at the time that I would one day have the privilege to help her share the inspirational story of her courageous life. Kim is devoted to her family and her faith; she demonstrates this daily in such humble ways. I admire her so much.

I'd also like to thank Brad Smith for his help. He's a supportive husband; he's also an incredible Dad. When I first learned he was dating Kim many years ago, I was hoping that he'd be her mate for life.

Kim would be the first to say that this book could have never been written without the guidance and unconditional love of her mother, Jackie. This is so true. Jackie was the compass who kept this book on course and I'm so appreciative of her strength.

Finally, I'd like to thank my junior high English teacher, Laura Coburn, the wise and compassionate woman who inspired me to be a teacher. Were it not for Mrs. Coburn, I might have missed out on pursuing a rewarding career that was filled with treasures like Kim Brinkman Smith.

Fitting In

On a crisp October morning in 1995, Kim was sitting in Sunday school. She didn't hear a word the teacher said. Like most sixteen-year-old girls, she would have rather skipped church and stayed in bed. For her parents, Jackie and Roger, missing church wasn't an option unless their daughters didn't feel well. Jackie, a professional nurse, always saw through their feigned illnesses that ironically seemed to fall on Sunday mornings. Sometimes it was all she could do not to laugh, especially when the girls expended so much effort in rehearsing their dramatic facial gestures that emoted, "I can't go to church today, Mom. My stomach hurts."

The four Brinkman sisters learned at an early age that the "I have a fever" excuse was futile. That simply led to their mother feeling their foreheads and saying in a cheerful tone that only aggravated them more, "You feel fine. Get dressed. It's a wonderful day." Granted, their mother had a beautiful singing voice but it didn't resonate well when she tried to perk them up with her gleeful song: "Good morning, good morning, good morning, it's time to rise and shine! Good morning, good morning, good morning, I hope you're feeling fine!"

Kim didn't even try to focus on the teacher's lesson because her mind was consumed with the essay she'd written for English class earlier in the week; the students were asked to write a short biographical sketch of their lives that included where they envisioned themselves ten years later. When the essays were returned, she received an 'A' with these words written at the top of the page: 'You have done a wonderful job in expressing your feelings, Kim. I hope your dreams come true.' The teacher's comment was encouraging support for this insecure teenager whose essay read:

Finding Me

I have always had this view since childhood that we were a perfect family. I can probably count on one hand the number of times I was punished as a little girl. Even though I argue with my sisters, we really don't fight to the point of being vicious. When you look at our family photo album, we're always smiling and everyone looks happy. The pictures are telling the truth; we are a close-knit, happy family. My sisters and I have been raised by extremely loving and caring parents. I wish I could insert some drama at this point and say that our smiles aren't genuine or that there's a dark secret lurking in our family but I can't.

I know I'm fortunate to have been raised in a Christian home where God is the foundation of my morals and beliefs. However, I'm more than reluctant to share this with my friends. If I talk about my faith, I'm afraid of being misunderstood and alienated. My friends are a very important part of my life and I am so desperate to feel like I fit in that I follow the crowd when I know it's often the wrong thing to do. This sometimes means lying to my parents about where I'm going on the weekends.

It's no secret that there are underage drinking parties somewhere in the county every weekend. Sure, I could stand up to the peer pressure. I could say, "I'd rather not go" when the truth is I want to go because I don't ever want to feel left out. I could say that I've never had a beer or puffed on a cigarette with my friends but that would be a lie. Even as I write this, I cringe in knowing this would disappoint my parents and people who respect me. I justify all this by telling myself repeatedly that this is all part of growing up and I don't need to feel guilty. Yet deep down I do because there is the other me who is very conscientious about my school work and my public image.

It wasn't until junior high that I realized friendship was more than a scary roller coaster ride. It was unforgiving as well, especially when I was the victim of cruel teasing. More times than I care to remember, I came home depressed and low on self-esteem. Regrettably, I was just as bad in hurting others' feelings in the fickle game we played. It's too bad we can't bypass our junior high years that are dictated by raging hormones and devastating peer pressure. This was the point in my life where I began to test the boundaries my parents had set.

As the oldest child, I've always been the guinea pig for my parents' rules, curfews and punishments. I resent not being allowed to stay out as late as my friends and this turns into anger that turns into feeling disconnected from my mom and dad at times. I once told them I was going to walk on the wild side whether they liked it or not. I didn't let it end there. I said I was tired of feeling like I've been led around on a leash and that I didn't want to behave like the perfect daughter.

I believe God is just standing on the sidelines saying, "Who are you trying to kid? Your parents have never expected you to be perfect. You have no one but yourself to blame for some bad decisions you've made. You aren't fooling anyone but yourself, Kim."

So where do I envision my life in ten years? I'm not nearly as career-minded as many of my friends. While I hope to have a job I enjoy, I'm far more focused on having a family. I dream of marrying a guy who will make me feel like we've just fallen in love every day of our lives. I want him to love the idea of being a parent as much as I do. I want him to have my dad's gentle nature and strong character. My greatest wish is to be a mother just like my mom. She is so compassionate, giving and steadfast in her faith. For this wish to come true, I need to figure out who the real Kimberlee Renee Brinkman is. I hope I meet her soon; maybe then I'll choose to follow a new path instead of this unstable one I'm on.

Kim couldn't help but smile amusedly at the ironic timing of the writing assignment. She felt like the topic was intended specifically for her. She even thought to herself, "If I didn't know better, I'd swear my teacher knew about the letter Mom gave me two weeks ago."

She reached for the letter in her purse that had been safely hidden from anyone else's view and unfolded it on her lap. She had read it so many times that she could nearly recite it. Without being conspicuous, she looked down and read it once again:

Dear Kim,

I am writing this personal letter to you from the bottom of my heart. I ask that it stays between the two of us. When the time comes for your sisters to hear this, I will ask the same of them. I know you have a hard time talking to us about guys and dating, so I've decided to share some feelings with you on paper. I bet right now you are saying, "Oh, my gosh!"

Kim, your dad and I love you so much. For 16 years, we have tried to nurture you, to guide you in your relationship with the Lord and to be respectful of others. I feel like we have the most wonderful family on this earth. God has blessed me with the most precious daughters and husband. Remember when I told you that I prayed often for my future husband, even before I started dating? I prayed for my future children as well. In the book of Psalms, the Bible tells us to delight in the Lord and He will give you the desires of your heart. God has answered my prayers and given me the desires of my heart.

Now it comes to you. I love you so much and want so much for you. When you were little, it was so easy to save you from life's hurts; you are now at a point in your life where I can't do that anymore. I realize that you wouldn't want me to if I could. That is how you grow. We have raised you with strong moral and Christian values but we can't live your life for you. It is time for us to loosen up and let you stretch your wings. We need to step back a bit and let you make your own decisions. Some will be right and some will be wrong but you will learn. It is so hard to let you do this. It isn't that your dad and I don't trust you because we do. Friends can be deceiving and make things look and sound so much better than they really might be. Of course, you will be curious and Dad and I can't say we were saints when we were your age.

We hope that you will always include us in your dating choices and involve the guys in our family activities. We are proud of our family and want your friends to see the love that dwells in our home. I pray for your future husband. You might as well know that I also pray God will help you stay pure sexually until after your marriage. This is not just because God asks us to in the Bible but because our bodies are gifts to give to our husbands on our wedding nights.

I know that I haven't always given in to what you want and that we've been strict. As our firstborn, it is so hard to let go but we will try! You'll understand exactly what I'm feeling when you're a mother one day. I think it's time to finish this letter to my favorite oldest daughter. We LOVE you very much and will always be here for you.

With Great Respect for a Very Special Daughter,
Love,
Mom

The Unknown

The next thing Kim knew, Sunday school was over. For no particular reason, she rubbed her neck and was instantly terrified when she felt the enlarged lymph node. Tears began to pool in her eyes. She quickly blinked them away and raced down the hall to find her mother.

Jackie was talking with friends at the back of the sanctuary when she heard the panic in Kim's voice.

"Mom, feel this lump! What is it? Something is wrong! Do you think it's serious?"

Jackie quickly quelled her fears. After she felt the visibly enlarged node, she disguised the heartbreaking suspicion that raced through her mind.

"Honey, did you accidentally get hit in the neck playing volleyball?"

"No, but last night after the game a bunch of us went uptown for pizza and someone jokingly jumped on my back. It pulled my neck back and really hurt."

"I don't know if that would cause a lump like this. Have you had a sore throat?"

"It's not really a sore throat but remember when I told you this summer that it felt swollen sometimes? It hurt when I was lying down but the pain left once I got up."

"I remember. Maybe it's an infected lymph node. I'll call the family doctor tomorrow to get it checked out."

"I wonder if I have mononucleosis; some kids at school have had it. I hope that's not it because I'd have to miss school and volleyball."

As the worship music began, the two of them joined their family in the pew. Kim's hands had finally stopped shaking and she felt relieved that her mother hadn't seemed upset by things. She whispered, "I bet this is no big deal, Mom. Maybe the doctor can just give me some medication and the lump will go away."

As tears and fears joined forces in Jackie's heart, she found the strength to conceal them. As the service continued, she silently prayed, *"Dear God, I don't have a good feeling about this. I pray that you will help us find the right doctors quickly. We need to know what it is and deal with it. I pray that this isn't what I'm thinking. In Jesus' name I pray. Amen."*

Normally, Jackie was never in a hurry to leave the sanctuary once church was over. She and Roger enjoyed the fellowship afterwards with friends. He sensed this Sunday morning was different but didn't know why. He made eye contact with her that signaled, "Are you okay?" and realized she was fighting back some serious tears. After 18 years of marriage, he knew they needed to talk privately. So as soon as dinner was over and the girls began cleaning up the kitchen, he looked at Jackie and said, "I'll be out in the shed. I have some work to do."

He was standing by the workbench when Jackie walked in minutes later. "Roger, there is something very wrong with Kim.

She has an enlarged lymph node on her neck. I know it's serious. We have to get this checked out as quickly as possible. I'm calling the doctor tomorrow morning."

Not knowing what to say, he looked down and shook his head in despair. He remembered how tough it was for him when his mother died at the age of 39. He was only 14 at the time. It wasn't until many years later that his older siblings told him their mother had died from some form of lymphatic cancer.

"Jackie, we're not going to talk about the 'what ifs' until we know what's wrong."

"I know," she cried. "I just pray my suspicions are wrong."

The Painful Reality

*J*ackie called the family physician's office as soon as it opened Monday morning. When the doctor learned of her concern, he said to bring Kim in right away. He examined her thoroughly and there was a certainty in his voice when he looked at Jackie and said, "This needs to be checked out by an ear, nose and throat specialist as soon as possible. The lymph node will need to be biopsied. Is there a particular specialist you prefer?"

Trying to keep her voice from trembling, Jackie said, "I'd like to have Dr. Robertson in Findlay. I work for a group of OB/GYN doctors and have heard many people say that he is excellent. Do you think it will take long to get an appointment with him?"

"I'm actually going to contact his office now. My hope is that he can examine Kim tomorrow. Let me see what I can do."

The doctor returned within 15 minutes. They had an appointment to see Dr. Robertson the next day. As soon as they got in the car, Kim said, "I'm not really sure I understood everything the doctor explained about biopsies. So there's a needle biopsy and a surgical biopsy?"

"That's right, honey."

"Well, I sure hope it's a needle biopsy because I don't want a surgery. That would leave a scar and the Homecoming dance is this weekend. I don't want everyone to see me wearing a bandage."

"We can't look that far ahead, Kim. Let's see what Dr. Robertson says." The whole time Jackie was saying this, she was thinking, "A scar is going to be the least of our worries if this turns out to be what I fear."

Once they arrived home, Kim grabbed her volleyball outfit and on the way out the door yelled, "Mom, I might be a little late getting home. I'm going to stop at the drugstore after practice and buy a new journal. I need to start writing some of this stuff down."

With supper cooking in the crock pot, Jackie went to the bedroom to lie down. She was feeling nauseous in thinking about the doctor's appointment the next day. Nervous fatigue ultimately prevailed and she fell asleep; she awakened two hours later to the sounds of Joy, Kari and Libby getting off the bus. When she got out of bed to greet them and to hear how their day had gone, her pillow was still damp from all the tears she didn't remember crying.

After Kim got home from practice, ate a good supper and showered, she went to bed later than usual because she had homework to catch up on. Jackie reminded her of the plan for the next day. Roger would leave work early to pick her up at school and Jackie would meet them at Dr. Robertson's office. Kim nodded her head. "I know, Mom. We've already talked about this."

Jackie couldn't sleep the entire night. She fought the nightmares playing out in her mind. She didn't know what to expect in terms of Kim's moods and reactions to everything that seemed horribly surreal.

Because of another early dismissal from school, Kim was in a visibly upset mood when she arrived at the doctor's office. Her frame of mind spiraled into total disgust when she walked into the waiting room that was filled with children, adolescents and adults. Turning to Jackie as if she really believed her mother could do something about it, she mumbled, "We'll have to wait at least 30 minutes or more. This is ridiculous! If there really is something wrong with me then why is it taking so long? I'm never going to make it back in time for the volleyball game."

No sooner had she said this than the nurse appeared and called her name. Kim jumped up quickly and expected her parents to follow but the nurse said, "Kimberlee, why don't you come with me and I'll help you get changed. Once Dr. Robertson is done with the exam, we'll have your parents join you."

While the nurse exchanged pleasantries in helping Kim put on the gown, Jackie's hands began to tremor visibly. She said in desperation, "Roger, Kim has no idea how serious this could be. The main thing on her mind is getting home in time to play volleyball." Roger reached over to hold her ice-cold hand and continued to look at the dark carpeting he'd been staring at for over an hour.

When they were called back, Kim was sitting on the examining table. Dr. Robertson had momentarily stepped out of the room. Jackie hugged her gently. "Are you holding up okay, honey?"

"Yeah, I am but I hate wearing a gown. Dr. Robertson checked me everywhere and kept asking if different lymph nodes hurt. I didn't know there are lymph nodes in your stomach and groin and under your armpits. When he touched the lump, he asked me to describe what it felt like. I said it was kind of numb and how my throat feels swollen at night when I'm in bed. I told him how much it hurt when my neck got pulled back the other night."

Just as Kim finished talking, Dr. Robertson walked into

the room. As he shook Jackie and Roger's hands and introduced himself, he made eye contact with Jackie that she perceived to be a warning for what was to come.

He looked at them with compassion. "Mr. and Mrs. Brinkman, I need to biopsy Kim's lymph node as soon as possible; we need to rule out Hodgkin's disease. In looking at the surgery schedule, I can do it Monday at Blanchard Valley Hospital. Kim, I want you to have blood work done at the hospital tomorrow; you'll also have x-rays and a CAT scan. Let's not jump to any conclusions until all the test results are in. Do you have any questions at this point?"

They didn't and Jackie thanked him for seeing them on such short notice. "Then go ahead and get dressed, Kim, while your parents pick up the necessary paperwork at the front desk. I'll see everyone Monday."

Kim immediately got in Jackie's car and encouraged her to drive faster; she wanted to get to school in time to watch most of the varsity volleyball game. Roger followed them home and assumed that Jackie was barraged with questions. Jackie anticipated the questions, too, as they pulled out of the parking lot. She purposely waited for Kim to talk first as she gathered her composure to respond to anything she asked.

"Mom, I'm disappointed I have to have surgery but I feel really comfortable with Dr. Robertson. I thought I'd be more nervous during the exam. He makes you feel like he really cares, doesn't he?"

"He does. Your dad and I liked him very much. We have a lot of faith in him."

"I wonder how much blood they'll draw at the hospital tomorrow. I hate needles. Is this going to hurt a lot? I hope I don't faint."

"You'll feel a little pinch when they draw your blood. You'll do fine."

"What is this CAT scan I'm going to have?"

"It's a very specific type of x-ray. It will tell Dr. Robertson if there are any other enlarged lymph nodes in your body. When you get home from the volleyball game, we can talk about all this in more detail. I've got a pot of vegetable soup made and want you to eat before you go to the game."

"I'll eat when I get home. I'm not hungry. I just want to see my friends."

"You've had a nerve-wracking day, young lady. You're going to eat before you go to the game and that's final."

Kim inhaled a bowl of soup and as she was hurrying out the door said, "Mom, what should I say about my appointment today if everyone asks?"

"Just tell the truth. Tell them that you're having more tests tomorrow."

Roger had stopped for gas on the way home. As he was pulling into the driveway, Kim was pulling out. He took this to be a good sign that she felt up to going to the game. He hadn't eaten much all day so the soup smelled inviting as he and Jackie sat at the table with their daughters. They reached out to hold one another's hands as Jackie prayed: *"Dear Heavenly Father, we give you thanks for bringing us together as a family tonight. Thank you for nourishing our bodies. We pray for Kim to have the strength she'll need to get through tomorrow's tests. In Jesus' name we pray. Amen."*

The girls were delighted after supper when Jackie said, "You don't have to help clean up the kitchen tonight. Dad and I will do it." As soon as the girls left, Roger asked, "Was Kim really upset on the way home?"

Jackie shrugged her shoulders. "She was amazingly calm. I still can't believe it. She asked a few questions about getting blood drawn and the CAT scan but other than that she didn't seem afraid. She never once talked about what will happen if she has Hodgkin's disease. It's almost like she's in denial that she might have cancer."

"Jackie, Dr. Robertson never used the word 'cancer' today and neither have we. Maybe she doesn't realize what Hodgkin's disease is."

Jackie's knees weakened. "Roger, I assumed she knew. What if she doesn't?"

"Then we need to tell her when she gets home."

He had hardly finished the sentence when they heard the car door slam. Kim came running into the house in hysteria yelling, "Mom, where are you?"

She fell into Jackie's arms and sobbed. "Someone at the game told me Hodgkin's disease is cancer. That's not right, is it?"

Roger felt helpless watching Jackie take a deep breath. "Kim, I'm so sorry. We thought you knew what the disease is. Otherwise, I would have told you immediately. Honey, it's a form of lymphatic cancer but we don't know if you have it. That's why Dr. Robertson ordered more tests."

Kim pulled away in shock and anger. "No one told me! You and Dad should have told me! People die from cancer!"

She ran to her bedroom and slammed the door. Jackie couldn't bear hearing her weep uncontrollably. She gently knocked on the bedroom door. "Honey, can Dad and I come in? Let's talk."

"No! There's nothing to talk about now. Just leave me alone."

They respected her need for privacy and went out on the deck in the hopes that Kim would eventually join them. Instead, she never left her room.

The Journal

Tuesday, October 3, 1995

I can't believe what I'm about to write. In three days I have gone from finding an enlarged lymph node on my neck to just learning tonight that Hodgkin's disease is cancer. I really yelled at Mom and Dad. They assumed I knew what Hodgkin's is and I didn't. I wouldn't let them come into my room to talk. I'm so upset and angry that I don't know who I even am. If I do have cancer, I wonder if I'll ever be the same again. I wonder how long I'll live. I'm so scared I can hardly write.

I felt paralyzed tonight when I heard the word 'cancer.' I thought I was going to throw up. My Grandpa Brinkman died from it and even though I was really young, I remember how much he suffered. I keep thinking that maybe this is just a cruel joke and tomorrow I'll wake up and the lump will be gone. I keep thinking, "WHY ME, GOD? I'm only sixteen. I've been healthy all my life. Am I supposed to learn something from all this? Are you trying to test my faith? Tell me!"

I just want to think about seeing my friends at school tomorrow, playing volleyball and getting a new outfit for the Homecoming dance. I look forward to cheering at the football game with my friends and eating pizza afterwards. Instead, I'm going to the hospital to have a bunch of tests that will help my doctor know if I have more enlarged lymph nodes hiding in my body. I feel like innocent prey that is ready to be attacked by a savage predator. If I do have Hodgkin's disease, I won't go down without a fight. I'm a competitor and I hate to lose.

Wednesday, October 4, 1995

I woke up as soon as Mom called me this morning. My stomach was bombarded with nervous butterflies I couldn't control. When she came into the kitchen, I gave her an extra long hug to apologize for getting so upset with her last night. She kissed me on the forehead and said, "You're going to do fine today, Kim. Once everything is over, you might feel a little light-headed but you'll perk up after you've eaten."

She was right. I did feel a little queasy after the CAT scan that involved being injected with a dye through an IV. While the machine was scanning my body, I kept thinking, "Don't throw up, Kim. You're not the first teenager to have this test." The chest x-ray and blood work went fine. I was just anxious to get home because I was excited about playing in the volleyball game tonight against Ft. Jennings.

I did ask Mom how soon we'd know the test results. I could tell she was trying to be really strong for me but her voice quivered when she said, "Tomorrow sometime. Dr. Robertson's office will let us know."

Those words "will let us know" give me chills. At this time tomorrow, I will know if I likely have Hodgkin's disease. I will know if I likely have cancer. I'm too scared to be angry. I feel abandoned by God. I feel like a lost child crying to be saved but no one hears me.

The Sunroom

Jackie was awake before dawn and quietly slipped out of bed and reached for her Bible and book of devotions on the nightstand. She tiptoed past the girls' bedrooms and went to the sunroom, her tranquil sanctuary. She normally looked forward to her morning ritual of prayer and meditation but this particular morning was different. Her heart was frozen in fear. At some point in the day, the phone would ring and she would have no choice but to answer it; she would have no choice but to learn the results of Kim's biopsy. She questioned how all this could be happening. Kim had rarely been sick a day in her life.

Within seconds her mind stepped out of the moment and retreated to that miraculous day on March 20, 1979, when Kim was born. She clearly remembered hearing the nurse say, "Mrs. Brinkman, you have a healthy 9 lb. 10 oz. daughter with beautiful black hair."

One sweet memory joined another. Jackie relived her daughter's childhood joy when they spent time together cooking and baking in the kitchen when Kim set up her own 'Won Fron's Cooking Show' on the counter. While holding a make-shift microphone, the young chef in short pigtails explained how to prepare certain foods to the TV audience. Then there were the days when this imaginative performer would grab two spoons and say, "Here's one for you, Mommy. Let's pretend they're microphones and sing together when I help you clean the house."

Clenching her Bible to her heart, Jackie poured out her anguish in prayer: *"Lord, I hand everything over to you. Why do we have to go through this? What good could possibly come from Kim having cancer? She's a teenager and has her whole life ahead of her. Why can't it be me instead? Let me bear her pain."*

In the silence that followed, she sat quietly before the Lord and was embraced by a spiritual stillness. She felt God say: *"Yes, Kim will have cancer but she will live. Her life will be a witness to many."*

The revelation penetrated her soul. Tears fell like heavy raindrops, the harbingers of bitter truth that their lives would never be the same. She remained motionless for several minutes and tried to comprehend what had just happened. When she heard Roger getting his breakfast, she tentatively walked into the kitchen.

"Honey, there is something I need to share with you." In a trembling voice that struggled to find the words, she described what she'd experienced. When she was finished, Roger held her and faithfully said, "Then now we know how to pray, Jackie. Now we know what we are fighting and we know we're not alone."

The Phone Call

Jackie dreaded going to work, even though she knew she'd be surrounded by supportive co-workers and doctors who were like family. She tried to envision how the day would go and none of the scenarios had a happy ending. She knew that at some point she would have to pick up the phone and hear the test results.

When she arrived at the office, her colleagues hugged her one by one; they searched in vain for the words that could console a mother who was awaiting horrific news. While everyone pretended to go about the day as if it were like every other, one of Jackie's secretaries volunteered to call Dr. Robertson's office because she had a friend who worked there. Through frightened tears, Jackie said, "I'd appreciate it so much."

The call was made. Jackie's co-worker talked with her friend who said the information was on Dr. Robertson's desk and he would call Jackie the first opportunity he had. Each time the phone rang, the staff held its breath. When it was someone calling to schedule an appointment, Jackie felt like she'd been given a reprieve – however short it might be.

Then the phone call came. She went into her office and closed the door. Her mouth was so dry she could barely say, "Hello." She listened as intently as possible when he explained that the CAT scan showed there was a great deal of lymph node involvement from Kim's diaphragm up to her neck. While the results indicated a high probability of Hodgkin's disease, the only way to be certain was to perform a biopsy.

Her co-workers could hear Jackie crying and when she didn't come out of her office for several minutes, one of her friends opened the door and said, "What can we do to help?"

"I need to leave right away," she sobbed. "Kim will get home in 45 minutes and I need to be there to tell her."

She raced home through the blinding tears that impaired her vision. She prayed between moments of trying to catch her breath; she felt like she was caught in a ravaging storm with no refuge in sight. Determined that Kim wouldn't see her in emotional shambles, she hurried into the house. As she washed her tear-stained face with a warm washcloth, she hoped that Kim wouldn't have a friend with her because they needed to be alone.

While she was trying to think how she'd phrase things, Kim and her good friend were on their way to pick up Kim's volleyball uniform. As soon as the house was in sight, Kim slowed down. "This isn't good, Natalie. Mom's car is home and she should be at work."

Jackie hurried to the door when she heard the car pull into the driveway. No words were spoken. In the shroud of silence, Jackie reached out to catch Kim whose legs faltered. Natalie stepped back.

"Mom," she cried, "it's really bad, isn't it?"

Jackie nodded her head and held Kim to her chest; they wept to the painful rhythm of their breaking hearts.

Once Kim's body stopped shaking and she caught her breath,

she reached out for Natalie's assuring hug of friendship. "I'm so sorry, Kim. I'm here for you."

"I know, Nat. I appreciate you so much. Let's go talk in my bedroom and figure out what I'm going to tell the coach and the team tonight."

As Jackie started fixing supper, she thought to herself, "Things seem to have a way of working out. Kim needed for Natalie to be here."

Just as Joy, Kari and Libby were getting off the bus, Kim and Natalie were leaving for the volleyball game but not before Jackie hugged them goodbye and thanked Natalie.

Jackie hadn't planned on telling the girls about Kim's health status until she first shared everything with Roger. Then they could tell them together. She had somewhat regained her composure but that changed when Roger got home from work and walked into the kitchen. She didn't want to scare the girls, so she reached for his hand and they walked into the garage. As Jackie struggled to tell him the test results, he held her and said, "Listen to me. We're going to take things one day at a time. Our faith will pull us through, Jackie. We're going to Kim's volleyball game after supper and we're going to keep everything as normal as possible." As he wiped away her lingering tears, she clung to her pillar of strength.

Before leaving for the game, she tried to conceal the left-over tears with makeup. In her mind, the efforts were in vain. The moment she and Roger stepped into the gymnasium, she felt like everyone was staring at her and whispering, "Jackie looks like she's been crying for days. Did you hear that Kim might have cancer?"

Kim had obviously shared her health issues with her coach and teammates and the news had spread rapidly. Even though people meant well, the weight of their sympathy was nearly unbearable. Jackie did her best to disguise what she was feeling and found herself cheering even louder than usual for the Lady Bulldogs, especially for Kim who played the best game of her volleyball career.

Anxiety

Thursday, October 5, 1995

What a day! I keep thinking there is an alias out there who is posing as 'the sick Kim Brinkman' I don't know. I feel strong right now and want to shout to everyone: "Hey, look at me! It's the real Kim. I'm the same person. I haven't changed. I know the news sounds grim but I will never give up! All I need are your prayers."

Before the volleyball game tonight, I went to the coach and told her about my situation. She hugged me and was just as caring as I knew she would be when I talked to my teammates before the game. I ran several speeches through my mind ahead of time. I wanted to find the easiest way to explain things without a lot of tears.

There was no easy way; so I just spoke from my heart and said, "As a captain of our team, I need to be honest and say that this will probably be the last volleyball game of the season I play with you. I just learned that there is a strong possibility I have Hodgkin's disease. It's cancer of the lymph nodes. I'm going to play to the best of my abilities tonight and I know you will too. Play this game for me but don't feel sorry for me. Keep thinking of me as your teammate. Even when I'm not physically able to compete with you, I'll be with you in spirit. I'll always be cheering for you to win."

The girls were stunned and stared at the floor. They were choked up and afraid to look at me or each other. Then they did what teammates do. They rallied with hugs of support. I'm really going to miss playing with them. I tell myself that I'll be back as strong as ever to play next year but deep down I have no idea what my health will be like a year from now or even a month from now.

Friday, October 6, 1995

I've looked forward to Homecoming week at school for so long. I got a new outfit for the dance that looks awesome. But instead of being able to stay in school all day and enjoy the pep rally with my friends, Dr. Robertson wanted to examine me again before he does the biopsy Monday. He thoroughly checked out the lymph nodes in my chest area, breasts, armpits, stomach and groin. Part of me thinks the biopsy will show cancer but another part of me thinks it won't because I feel good and look healthy. I'm really scared. I've even wondered if this might be my last Homecoming dance or if I'll still be alive in April to go to prom. I can't tell anybody what I'm thinking because it would just upset them and me even more.

Before Mom and Dad went to my volleyball game last night, they told my sisters what was happening. They really don't understand how serious this might be. They're too young. Hey, I'm sixteen years old and I don't understand. I know one thing for sure. Mom and Dad will do everything they can to remind them of our faith. This is our anchor and it's who we are.

This is how I want to raise my children one day – to walk the same Christian path my parents have paved for us. I'm a long way from staying on the path right now in my relationship with Christ. I think I'll get there eventually. It would help if God could give me even a little sign that I'm going to survive and that He'll never leave me.

Sunday, October 8, 1995

Homecoming was great. A bunch of us girls spent the night at a friend's house; we had fun sneaking out and going to a party that my parents don't know about. When Mom picked me up for church this morning, she wanted to hear about the dance but I was too tired to talk about it. I got choked up when I saw how red and puffy her eyes were. This should have been a warning that church was going to be very emotional for everyone.

I lost it when Pastor Jim asked the whole congregation to pray for me. Although it did catch me off-guard, I wasn't embarrassed. I felt comforted that so many people were praying for me at that same moment in time.

I couldn't believe all the phone calls from people tonight who are praying for my surgery to go well. There were a lot of hugs when my friends stopped in to say how much they care about me. Some of them cried and that made me cry. It really makes a difference when you know how much you matter to others. I'm thankful for this. I'm also very afraid of what's going to happen tomorrow.

The Waiting Room

It was a 40-minute drive to the hospital that was punctuated with an uncomfortable silence. Jackie finally turned around to Kim and said, "We can talk about the surgery if you have questions running through your mind."

"Yeah, I do have a question. If I'm just having a simple biopsy, why do I have to be there so early before the surgery? I could have slept in a little longer. Plus I'm hungry and can't believe I'm not allowed to eat anything!"

"There will be a lot of papers to fill out and the anesthesiologist will want to talk to you."

Kim looked away in nervous disgust and stared out the window muttering, "I can't believe I'm not allowed to wear makeup and had to take off my nail polish. This is so stupid."

Roger hadn't said anything up to that point but seized the opportunity to lighten the moment. "Really, Kim, I hadn't noticed you don't have makeup on? I thought you always looked like this."

His strategy worked. The tension eased when Kim instantly quipped, "Dad, that was mean!"

Within minutes, they pulled up to the outpatient surgery

entrance and reluctantly got out of the car. Once inside the hospital, things moved quickly. A nurse extended a warm greeting and introduced herself as she escorted them to the room; she reassured Kim that she would be with her throughout the surgery.

"I'll need for you to change into this very attractive hospital gown while I get your chart ready." Kim couldn't help but laugh. "Not one of those gowns again! It looks like the one in Dr. Robertson's office."

When the nurse returned, she began to go over everything that would be happening prior to and after the surgery. By the time she was finished, Kim could feel her body begin to relax from the medication she'd been given. She no longer felt nervous and watched the nurse insert the IV. It was a precautionary measure in case medication was necessary during surgery.

She felt even more relaxed when the nurse explained, "After your surgery, Kim, you will need to stay in the recovery room for a while. We will monitor your vitals and then we'll bring you back to the room where your parents will be waiting for you. Once you're able to keep some food down and go to the bathroom on your own, you'll be released to go home and recuperate."

As Jackie listened intently to the nurse's words, she was struck by the irony that she had said some of these very same things to her patients over the years. She found herself thinking, "You do see our precious daughter, don't you? You do see how scared we all are. Thank you for being so kind to Kim and for answering all her questions."

Dr. Robertson came into the room quickly and once again went over the surgical procedure and answered any remaining questions before heading to surgery. The minute he left the room, Jackie looked at Roger. "They're coming to get her now. We need to pray."

Kim held her parents' hands and could feel her dad's strength as he prayed, *"Dear God, we pray for Kim's peace and for the doctors and nurses who will be with her during surgery. We pray for their wisdom and knowledge throughout the procedure. Whatever the outcome may be, we pray that we are prepared by your strength. In Jesus' name we pray. Amen."*

As the orderly walked into the room, they kissed her forehead and said in unison, "Love you." Although she tried to be brave, Kim couldn't stop the tears from trickling down her cheeks. As she was wheeled down the hall, she closed her eyes and silently prayed, *"Lord, please be with Dr. Robertson and the nurses during my surgery. I'm so scared. Please let your presence be with me. Amen."*

Once she was rolled into the surgery suite, Kim's fears were intensified by the sterile white walls and antiseptic smells that permeated the room; everyone was wearing green scrubs and masks that made it difficult to hear what was being said. Then she saw her Aunt Juleen and felt a sense of relief; Jackie's sister, who had often worked in surgery assisting the doctors where she was employed, had been given permission to be with Kim prior to the beginning of the procedure.

As she covered her niece's visibly shivering body with a blanket from the warming unit, Kim reached out for her hand. "Thank you, Juleen. It really means a lot to me that you're here."

She loved Kim like a daughter and gently patted her hand while trying to stave off the tears. "I'm going to be right here holding your hand until you fall asleep. Then I'll see you when you wake up. I love you." Those were the last words Kim heard before she fell into a deep sleep.

Once she left the surgical room, Juleen quickly wiped away

the tears and headed to the waiting room to be with Jackie and Roger. From a distance, she could hear them talking to Pastor Jim who had come to pray with them and be by their side until the surgery was over.

Before joining them, she quietly prayed, *"Lord, I have hoped that I could in some way be support for my sister and Roger. Instead, their peaceful spirits strengthen me. How do they do this? They call you their friend and know what your word promises. They stand on it. I'm so thankful for their relationship with you. I have faith that they will get through this as a family."*

Small talk filled the waiting room while everyone's mind was on Kim. Although Jackie and Roger appeared calm outwardly, their hearts were pounding. Roger constantly looked at his watch; one hour had passed. Shortly thereafter, the nurse walked in and said Kim was doing well in recovery and that it was time to return to her room where Dr. Robertson would talk to them.

Anguish hovered over them. Roger couldn't look at Jackie when she wiped away tears from her chapped lips. They felt like they were awaiting a final verdict. Within minutes, Dr. Robertson arrived. He explained that instead of one lymph node being involved, there were three that were entangled with one other; he said that he was nearly certain the pathology report would confirm Hodgkin's disease. He felt that the trauma to Kim's neck several days earlier had dislodged the nodes and made them visible for him to examine. Had this not happened, the cancer could have progressed even more by going undetected.

Jackie and Roger were utterly numbed by the news; they were speechless and afraid to ask if they could lose her to the disease. When he said he wanted to see Kim back at his office in two days to check her incision, Jackie nodded and reached for his hand.

"Thank you, Dr. Robertson, for taking such good care of our daughter."

Seconds after he left, the orderly transported Kim to her room. Although she was awake, her eyelids were heavy and her memory was hazy. "I feel like I've been asleep for days," she mumbled. "It was cold in the recovery room; the nurse kept covering me up with more blankets. She said I did great. What did Dr. Robertson say? Tell me the truth, Mom."

Jackie answered in a soothing tone. "The surgery went well. He found three lymph nodes that were tangled together instead of one."

"How much worse can this get?" Kim cried. "I bet my incision is really big. I know I'll have a scar. How long do I have to wear this bandage? It's heavy and feels like it's pulling my skin apart."

"Dr. Robertson wants to check your incision in two days to make sure everything is healing."

As a single tear teetered on her lower eyelash, Kim looked directly into Jackie's eyes and asked the inevitable. "Do I have cancer for sure, Mom?"

Jackie kissed her forehead and held her hand before answering. "There is a strong possibility you do. We won't be certain until the pathology report comes back tomorrow."

"So now we have to wait another day? Unbelievable! I just want to know so I can do whatever it takes to get better. Take me home. I hate this place and I hate my life!"

As they helped her sit up, she became light-headed. In spite of Jackie wanting her to lie down, Kim refused. "I just need to sit here and I don't feel like talking."

Thirty minutes later, she had eaten a little bit and said she could get dressed on her own. She quickly realized she wasn't strong enough and relented.

"Mom, will you help me? It's pretty sad when I can't even dress myself."

They weren't more than three miles from the hospital when Kim fell asleep in the backseat. Upon arriving home, they helped her out of the car and wrapped their arms around her waist; her wobbly legs were too weak to carry her exhausted body.

She was sound asleep within minutes of being helped into her pajamas and tucked in bed. Jackie shut the bedroom door, knowing the girls would soon be home from school filled with questions. For the next few hours, the three sisters took turns peeking into Kim's room and checking on her while Jackie contacted family members and friends. The phone never stopped ringing the rest of the night.

The Second Phone Call

*A*lthough Jackie had given Kim some pain medication that helped her sleep through the night and late into the morning, she wasn't expecting to feel so worn out and uncomfortable when she finally opened her eyes.

"Mom, I didn't think I'd feel this bad. This bandage really itches and I'm still a little dizzy."

"You're still feeling some of the effects of the anesthetic and pain from the incision. I'm going to fix you some breakfast and then you can get in our bed and watch TV."

She was so weak that Jackie had to all but carry her into the kitchen. "Mom, I'm so tired. I can't do anything without getting short of breath."

"You have to remember that you went through a lot yesterday."

Kim lashed out with all the sarcasm and anger she could muster. Her words pierced Jackie's already aching heart. "Really? Do you think I can actually forget I had surgery and went through a lot yesterday? Do you think I don't remember what's happened to me in the past two weeks?"

Slamming her plate on the table, she yelled, "Why can't I

have someone else's life right now? This isn't fair!"

"I'm sorry, Kim," were the only words Jackie could say. She felt so helpless as a mother. This time she couldn't fix things; she couldn't promise Kim that her life would ever be the same again. "You're right, honey. It isn't fair."

As Kim slowly got up from the table and headed towards the bedroom, she looked defeated. "Yeah, I know it isn't fair and I can't do anything about it, can I? I feel like someone else is living inside me. I wonder if I'll ever get 'me' back. I can't talk about this anymore."

Fifteen minutes later, Kim yelled, "Mom, I'm afraid to be alone. Will you stay with me?" Jackie crawled in bed and wiped away the frantic tears running down Kim's pale cheeks. "Honey, I'll stay with you all day. I'm not going anywhere."

"I'm sorry I yelled at you. I'm just so afraid. I'm having trouble catching my breath. I know the phone is going to ring and it's going to be bad news. I feel like God is trying to punish me."

"Punish you? Honey, why would you ever think that?"

"Maybe for the times I've lied to you and Dad and made bad decisions."

Before Jackie could assure her she wasn't being punished, Kim asked the question that hung in the air like suffocating smog.

"Mom, am I going to die?"

Jackie reached out to hold her. "I need to share something with you. I've been waiting until I felt the time was right. I was alone in the sunroom one morning last week and felt God's presence. My heart heard Him say that you would have cancer but would survive it."

Kim quickly pulled away and virtually shouted, "Do you really believe that?"

Jackie's emotions overflowed. She sobbed as she held her child. "I believe it with all my heart."

Kim wanted to comfort her by saying she believed everything she'd just heard when she really didn't. Not knowing what else to do, she clung to Jackie with every ounce of her diminished strength. "I love you, Mom. I know you trust God with my life."

Then the phone rang.

The Next Step

Tuesday, October 10, 1995

Well, we got the call from Dr. Robertson. He confirmed what we all knew deep down. I have cancer. Did I really just say that? Yes, I have cancer. Just 11 days ago, I felt the lump in my neck and now my life is in question.

I don't know what I would do without my mom. She seems to know exactly when I need her to hold me and listen to my fears. I hate what having cancer is doing to my family. It's tearing everyone up. Mom and I cried so hard together today, especially when she told me what Dr. Robertson said. I feel sorry for my sisters. They are all so quiet because they don't know what's happening. When they look at me, I can see in their eyes what they're thinking but are afraid to ask. They want to know if I'm going to be okay. I'm wondering the same thing. Right now that hope of one day being okay again is vanishing quickly.

I'm glad Mom told me about her spiritual moment in the sunroom. She sounds certain when she said she felt God's presence and heard Him say that I would survive. I trust her completely and know she wouldn't have said this unless she really experienced it.

I've never had God talk to me like that. I don't know anyone else who has. I've always prayed but I've never really taken the time to listen to what He might be saying. Mom always takes the time to listen. I wish I could do that. Even though I felt a little bit of relief after she shared everything, I still don't know why it has to be me.

I have so many great friends. They're all worried about me. I called Tara tonight and told her I have cancer. She came over immediately and started bawling. I had to calm her down. She told me that Brad started crying when he heard about everything I was going through. Even though we only dated a few months last summer before we broke up, it made me feel good to know he cared.

I have to get my incision checked tomorrow and Dr. Robertson is going to tell us when I'll see an oncologist. I didn't even know what an oncologist was until now. It's a cancer doctor who is going to set up a treatment plan for me. I have no idea what this will be. I just know I'm petrified.

Wednesday, October 11, 1995

I almost fainted today when Dr. Robertson took off my bandage. I couldn't believe all the stitches. My incision is probably three inches long. He said it's healing nicely but I keep wondering how it's going to look the rest of my life – however long that will be! I have to go back Monday to get the stitches out. When we leave his office, we go to the oncologist. I'm going to try and go back to school tomorrow for half a day. I'm really worried about falling behind in my classes.

Tara called tonight and said she was bringing over someone to surprise me. It was Brad and some of his friends. It was pretty awkward at first because no one knew what to say. I don't blame them. I wouldn't know what to say to someone either. I haven't really talked to anyone who has cancer. Brad was quieter than usual and didn't act macho like he did when we were dating. Maybe there is a softer side to him I've never seen. I guess I'll never know. I have to admit it was fun being with him at all the parties. Part of me liked his wild side.

Monday, October 16, 1995

I felt like crap this past weekend. I've been having hot and cold flashes lately. I don't know if it's from the cancer or if I'm coming down with something. I felt good enough to go to church yesterday. Dan Stechschulte felt led to pray for me. I stayed composed through it and held back the tears. I'm glad he did this. I know I need all the prayers I can get.

I had severe stomach aches last night and still felt awful today but went to school anyhow. I left shortly after lunch to go to Dr. Robertson's to get my stitches removed. When he took them out, it pulled where the scabs are. Even though he said the incision was healing, I thought it looked gross.

Then we had an appointment with the oncologist at 3 o'clock. So once again I had to wait a long time. I'm getting really fed up with all this. I probably should start paying more attention to the sign my great-aunt Marilyn gave me last week that says: 'God intends to teach me patience...if it takes Him an eternity!' Maybe this testing of my patience is what God's trying to tell me during this nightmare.

The oncologist was really nice. She asked a lot of questions. Did I recently have any weight loss? (No, I wish I had! I haven't weighed this much ever. I keep chalking it up to the weight lifting I've done for volleyball.) Did I have any appetite changes? (No.) Did I have any fevers, headaches or night sweats? (No. I didn't really say anything about the hot/cold sweats that I had this weekend since she specifically asked about the night sweats.)

She also examined all of my lymph node areas. She thought she found a few more that might be suspicious. We had to schedule more tests for the upcoming days. That's when she told me she had "to stage my cancer." This sent ice cold chills through me, especially when she said we needed to know where all the cancer was. That phrase "staging my cancer" sounded to me like "figuring out if I would live and for how long."

She mentioned the possibility of only needing radiation if the cancer hasn't spread too much or chemo if it's in more areas. I hate that word 'chemo.' I feel disgusted when I say it. I'm praying that I only have to do radiation. I can't help but wonder if my life will ever be close to normal. It's unfair that I can't even go to school for a full day right now.

I'm haunted by the things I learned today. Hodgkin's disease is also called Hodgkin's lymphoma. It's a cancer of the lymph tissue found in the lymph nodes, spleen, liver and bone marrow. The first sign is often painless swelling of lymph nodes in the neck, armpits or groin. It can spread to nearby lymph nodes and if my disease progresses, it will affect my body's ability to fight infection. Some of the other symptoms are fever and chills; night sweats; loss of appetite; weight loss and itchy skin. My disease is most often diagnosed in people between the ages of 15 and 35 and in people who are older than 55. When I learned that the cause is unknown, I wanted to scream, "Tell me about it! I wake up every day and wonder why this evil is growing in my body."

There are four stages of Hodgkin's lymphoma. Stage 1 means one group of lymph nodes is affected. By Stage 2, two or more groups of lymph nodes on the same side of the diaphragm are involved. In Stage 3, lymph nodes on both sides of the diaphragm are affected. By Stage 4, other parts of the body outside of the lymph system have been affected.

I am praying so hard that I have Stage 1. But what if it isn't? Mom knows I'm feeling extra depressed and extra scared. She gave my sisters and me these really neat signs tonight with our names written in cool calligraphy. Mine says 'Kim' in dark bold lettering and underneath is the meaning of my name which is 'Lady of Honor.' At the bottom is this Biblical verse from the book of Proverbs: 'Strength and honour are her clothing; and she shall rejoice in time to come.'

I cried so hard when I read it. I guess I really needed a good cry. I've tried to be strong through this but I can only do so much. I understand now what people mean when they say they've been blindsided. That's how I feel. I'm going to memorize this Bible verse and pray I have a future when I can 'rejoice in time to come.'

Tuesday, October 17, 1995

I'm beginning to realize that it doesn't do any good to anticipate what my day is going to be like. I knew Dad was going to pick me up *for an early dismissal but I didn't tell my friends that I was going to have this particular test. I knew they'd ask questions that I wouldn't know how to answer. The only thing I knew for sure was that the test would be painful. I took a pill called Ativan before leaving school. This seemed simple enough when I felt it sliding down my throat. It was supposed to help me relax and feel less nervous before the bone marrow test.*

If the anxiety from all this wasn't bad enough, I first had to go to the hospital and have an injection of radioactive gallium for my body scans that were scheduled for Thursday and Friday. These scans will determine where the cancer has gathered in my body. I can't think about this test right now because I'm so nervous about the bone marrow test. I can't think beyond the moment. Mom left work early and met us at the hospital. She hugged me the second I got out of the car. She looked so sad and worried.

No one should ever have to endure a bone marrow biopsy. Mom and Dad couldn't be with me for the test. Yes, the doctor and nurses did a good job of explaining the procedure minutes before it began but I had no idea the pain would be so excruciating. When they withdrew the marrow from two sites on the top of my hip bones, I felt like I was going to pass out or throw up. It felt like pieces of my soul were being extracted. Then they took samples of my bone. I was in so much gut-wrenching agony that I barely had the strength to plead, "I want my mom and dad" as torrential tears poured down my cheeks. I will never forget today as long as I live.

Wednesday, October 18, 1995

When I got up this morning, the first thing I did was peel off the bandages from my hips. I got light-headed immediately. I wasn't expecting to still see the two holes that are reminders of my cancerous enemy that is just waiting to take me down and leave scars behind. What is going to be left of my body when this is over?

Friday, October 20, 1995

I went to school this morning even though I'm still in pain from the biopsy. It hurts when I bend over. My friends are so sympathetic and supportive. So are my teachers. Everyone keeps asking me how I'm doing. I smile and say, "I'm okay" when I'm really not.

Talk about timing. I saw a book on one of my teacher's desk called 'When Bad Things Happen to Good People.' I don't need to read it because I already know what it's about. I'm living it! I bet the main character is a good person like me who can't understand why these bad things have happened. I wonder if the good person dies.

My Grandma Oglesbee picked me up at noon and drove me to the hospital for my Gallium scan. This really sucks because now I'm dealing with the effects of the laxatives I had to take earlier. The scan itself was easy but boring. I had to lie there and not move when the machine scanned areas where the gallium had settled ... areas that might be filled with cancer. I also had to have CAT scans of my abdomen and pelvic area. For the first time since all this began, I was able to watch the technician put the needle in my arm, knowing that my body was being filled with a contrast dye. I didn't grimace a bit. I'm actually beginning to feel numb from all the poking and prodding.

Grandma gave me a 'footprints pin' today. She got them for all the ladies in our family. It's really neat. It's gold and looks like three footprints of someone walking. It reminds me of the 'Footprints in the Sand' poem by Mary Stevenson that I've always loved. It carries even more meaning for me now. I feel like I'm the person in this poem who questions the Lord's presence and support. My favorite part of the poem is when the Lord reminds the person that the extra set of footprints in the sand are His and that even when it might not feel like it, He is always carrying us.

Tuesday, October 24, 1995

The results are in. I have Stage 2 Hodgkin's lymphoma. It's not exactly something that rolls right off the tip of the tongue. The cancer is in my neck and chest areas. All the lymph nodes involved are above the diaphragm.

I have a 75% chance of survival. I looked away when the oncologist said this. I didn't even hear the questions Mom asked because I pretty much escaped into a pretend world where the cancer can't touch me. I didn't even cry when I heard the final diagnosis. Maybe I'm worn out from crying. What was I supposed to say when I heard I have a 75% chance of living? How about "Well, I guess it's better than nothing!" I'm just so sick and tired of all this crap.

My oncologist is referring me to a state-of-the-art pediatric oncology unit. I know this makes sense because of my age. I looked away when she said, "Kim, a team of doctors will explain the course of treatment that will probably include chemotherapy and radiation."

I thought about our neighbor who died this week. His visitation is tomorrow. I wonder who will come to my visitation? How many will come and what will I be wearing in my casket?

Even though I've had some pretty bad headaches the last few days and am really tired, I perked up tonight when Tara and Brad came over. He brought me a stuffed animal. It was a brown dog that was holding a red pillow in the shape of a heart in its mouth. I was shocked when I saw what was hanging from the dog's neck. It was a beautiful garnet necklace. I love it!

I remember saying, "Brad, this is so pretty. I don't know what to say." He grinned and said, "I thought it might cheer you up." Tara just stood there and smiled.

I can't imagine how much money he had to spend on it. He certainly didn't have to give me something like this. Even though I always made it sound like it was mutual for both of us when we broke up last summer, it was really me who broke it off. Truthfully, I just can't see us being together in the future. He's already graduated and I want the freedom to date other guys while I'm still in school.

I can't picture us getting back together again but there were moments tonight when I felt like he still has feelings for me. Maybe I'm reading too much into his gift and the sensitive look in his eyes. I am sure of one thing. Today has been one of the worst days of my life and Brad is the only person who made me smile.

The Melody of Prayer

*K*im's headaches and stomach discomfort had subsided enough that she felt up to going to church with her family on the last Sunday morning in October. By now the majestic colors of autumn were stripped from the trees and chilly weather had arrived. The dreary day reflected Kim's depressed mood; she had trouble concentrating on anything but her doctor's appointment in Toledo that was scheduled for the following morning.

Within a few minutes after the Brinkmans settled into the pew, Jackie stood up and walked to the front of the sanctuary. Kim and her sisters all looked at each other with surprise. They always knew in advance when their mother was going to be part of special music during the worship service; in fact, they always looked forward to hearing her amazing voice that harmonized so well. The girls would often say, "Mom, how can you do that?"

Hoping to be let in on the secret, the girls looked at their dad. He purposely didn't make eye contact with them but did smile ever so slightly; this piqued their curiosity even more. As Jackie walked towards the microphone, Kim's pulse was racing with anxiety. Her mother never wanted to be in the spotlight; she always declined to sing solos for that very reason. Kim was tempted to stand and brazenly ask, "Mom, what are you doing?"

With newfound strength, Jackie looked at the congregation and said, "Roger and I are so thankful for all of you who are praying for Kim and our family. Your prayers sustain us and help us get through each day. We appreciate your support and kindness so much. I'd like to sing a song I heard on the radio when I was driving to work last week. I'd normally be shaking in fear to sing alone but today I'm unafraid because God has led me to this moment. This song is a reminder to all of us that even when we think we can't go on, God is always standing in the gap to carry us through."

As the music began, Jackie turned towards her family and said, "This song is dedicated to you, Kim. We are all praying and standing in the gap for you."

Before falling asleep that night, Kim praised God for the heartwarming worship experience. *"Dear Lord, thank you for the many people who are praying for me. Thank you for my friends and family whose support is endless. Thank you for giving Mom the strength to sing so beautifully in church. I will cherish that moment always. Tomorrow is another crucial day in my life that is filled with uncertainty. I'm beginning to feel strengthened by your presence and less afraid. I know that you and my parents will never let go of my hand. Regardless of my fears, I know in my heart that I will never be alone."*

The Unheard Voice

Kim stared out the backseat window the entire way to the hospital. When cars carrying teenagers passed them, she carried on a private conversation in that crevice of her mind where resentment lingered.

She found herself looking at the strangers and thinking, "I wonder where you guys are going? I bet it's somewhere fun. I'm going to the hospital. You've probably never worried that you could get cancer at your age. I didn't either until now."

Jackie's mind wandered too. She felt like they were driving into the trepid unknown. While she loved being a nurse, it had become a detriment when Kim was diagnosed; she knew too much about the potentially dire consequences that she couldn't verbalize to anyone but Roger. The closer they got to the hospital, the more she replayed the conversation they'd had earlier that morning.

"Jackie, we have to be really strong for Kim today."

"I know that but when we leave the hospital today, we'll probably be given an outline of the agony she'll go through for the next several months. She has no idea what the chemo will do to her body. None of us do. We can't protect her. My heart breaks when I think about it. You know how much she loves being around children. Her dreams are to get married and have a family. I keep asking God what all her dreams mean now. Her emotions are so fragile; I'm not sure how much more she can take. It's so important that the consultation with the doctor goes well."

Hospital entrances had become Kim's foes. She hated the ominous sound of the automatic doors that opened to sterile lobbies and sick people. Much to Jackie and Roger's surprise, Kim uttered, "This place doesn't look so bad. Maybe things will go better than I think."

There was endless paperwork for Jackie to complete. Kim paid attention to the countless insurance-related questions for the first time since being diagnosed.

"Mom, what would we do if Dad didn't have medical insurance?"

"Well, we need to be very thankful he does."

"I know but what if we didn't have any?"

"Then your dad and I would spend every cent we had to get you the best possible doctors and treatments available."

Before Kim could ask more questions, they were directed to the waiting room of the pediatric oncology department. She grew faint when she saw a few children clutching their favorite blankets or stuffed animals. They were all bald and one child was begging his mom to take him home.

"I feel so sorry for these kids. Mom, they look really sick. I wonder what kind of cancer they have. I could be a lot worse off than I am. I'm not going to stare at them. I wouldn't like it if people stared at me."

Within a few minutes, Kim's name was called. As they were led to the examining room, she prayed, *"Lord, please let the doctor say I don't need to have chemo."*

The moment the oncologist walked into the room, Jackie's hopes of a positive consultation were dashed. As he introduced himself and shook their hands, he never once made eye contact and didn't ask Kim any questions during the examination.

It took every ounce of restraint for Jackie not to say, "Sir, this is our teenage daughter. Could you at least look at her as a person? Could you at least show some feelings after telling her she has a 75% chance of surviving? She's a young girl who has been given a very bleak future. You're acting like she's supposed to just toughen up and get over it!"

Following the exam, the doctor said exactly what Kim didn't want to hear. "I've had a chance to review your records. You have signed up to be part of a clinical trial that will mean four months of chemotherapy. As part of the trial's protocol, your name could be pulled for follow-up radiation treatments that would take another month. You'll be under the care of a team of doctors, nurses, technicians and social workers. Someone on the staff will go over things in more detail in setting up a schedule for your chemo treatments. We also need to run more tests today. You'll need to schedule a date as soon as possible for a port to be surgically implanted beneath the skin in the chest area. This is how the chemotherapy drugs will be administered. Do you have any questions?"

In spite of being stunned by his distant demeanor, Jackie asked what side effects they should expect from the chemo. He reeled off an answer that he had obviously repeated many times. "Your daughter will lose her hair, be sick and have mouth sores. She'll lose weight from the chemo but will get a fat, round face from the steroids. More than likely, she will not be able to have children because of the caustic nature of the treatments."

Kim began to cry the second he left the room. Roger continued to clench the seat of the chair. He was in disbelief that a doctor could deliver so much bad news without showing any regard for her feelings and fears. Jackie temporarily withheld her frustration, knowing that she would be discussing this with one of the nurses when the time was right. Her priority at the moment was comforting Kim.

"Mom, he never even said my name. He probably doesn't know my name! He just looked at his stupid papers. He made me feel like I was a nuisance. He didn't care what I was thinking and acted like I wasn't even in the room!"

She had never seen her dad look so angry. "I feel like giving up, Dad. I don't think I can do this."

She hardly finished her sentence before he cut her off. "Yes, you can do this and you will. Giving up is not an option. You're a Brinkman and in case you haven't noticed, we are very strong-willed."

"Dad, you're putting it mildly. Brinkmans are just plain bull-headed."

"Now wait a minute," Jackie interjected. "The Brinkmans don't get all the credit. My side of the family can be just as bull-headed, so don't give your dad's family all the credit for your strong-willed personality, young lady!" Kim laughed out loud for the first time in days.

The rest of the day went better. Despite being overwhelmed and exhausted from the consultation, Kim understood why a battery of scans, x-rays, lab work and pulmonary function tests were necessary. Her team of doctors needed to establish a baseline before starting the chemotherapy treatments they wanted to begin as soon as possible. By the end of the day, she was worn out and welcomed the opportunity to sit down with the oncology nurse and social worker to discuss her treatment plan.

They were patient and compassionate in answering Jackie's many questions. Knowing that her mother understood what the treatment protocol would be was such a relief because Kim was too weary to listen. Then the nurse asked if she had any specific questions they hadn't answered.

She didn't hesitate to respond. "I'm not sure I totally understand my chemo schedule. It sounds like I come to the hospital on a Monday and have the drugs through IV therapy. On Tuesday through Sunday, I take chemo pills at home. Then I come back to the hospital the next Monday for IV therapy again and take chemo pills on Tuesday through Sunday. After that I get two weeks off completely. It means having two weeks of chemo and two weeks off, right?"

The nurse assured her she was right and asked if she had any other questions. "I do. It's probably the same one everybody else asks. Will I definitely lose all my hair?"

"With the type of chemotherapy treatment you'll have, Kim, you will lose all your hair. As upsetting as this is, keep reminding yourself that all your hair will grow back when your treatments are over."

"That feels like a million years away right now. Do you think I'll still have some of my hair by Christmas?"

"I can't tell you exactly when you'll lose all of it because everyone is different. I can tell you that it's extremely unlikely you'll have it by Christmas. Don't be surprised if it starts falling out before Thanksgiving."

There was nothing else to say. Kim was ready to go home;

she couldn't take more bad news. The minute they got in the car, she said, "Mom, I'm getting a wig immediately." She was sound asleep fifteen minutes later.

Jackie quietly said to Roger, "This still doesn't seem real. Kim's worried about losing her hair and we're worried about losing her."

"I know," he sighed.

A Kindred Spirit

Monday, October 30, 1995

Yesterday was a major setback. Nothing went the way I hoped. The oncologist I saw should seriously learn how to treat people. I don't care how smart he is. He has no bedside manner at all. Mom had a chance to talk with one of the nurses. I hope I have different doctors for the rest of my appointments.

I have surgery Wednesday. The doctor is going to put something in my chest called an internal port for the chemo treatments. The drugs are so strong that they can't be run through the veins of my arms in fear of damaging them. The port will be connected to a major vein in my body where the chemo will circulate. They can draw blood through the port so I won't have to be poked with needles all the time. I have a folder of information that explains the pros of a port but it's so complicated I'm not going to read it. It's too depressing. Besides, I can't do anything about it. I just know I'll have another scar to add to my body. As much as I hate the thought of more scars, I hate it even more when I think about losing my hair.

I cried a lot in school today. I know this surprised everyone because

I've been able to put up a brave front until now. I just couldn't pretend that I'm doing fine. While my classmates and I were talking about our quiz scores in Geometry, I was really thinking, "You know, there are a lot worse things in life to worry about than low quiz scores." I guess I'm learning the hard way what really matters in life and what doesn't.

I asked Tara and Natalie to go with me tomorrow to get my hair cut. I need them for moral support. I've spent years waiting for my hair to be this long and now I'm going to get it cut all one length, just below my shoulders. I've read about people who shave their heads before starting chemotherapy. I can't stand the thought of losing my hair that way. That time will come soon enough anyhow.

The best part of today was receiving a letter from a girl named Cheri who had Hodgkin's lymphoma. My Aunt Juleen knows her. I really appreciate this girl caring enough to take the time to write. Some of the things she's said are very bitter pills to swallow. It helps to know that I'm not the only one going through Hodgkin's.

Kim,

Your Aunt Juleen sent me a letter regarding you this week. Five years ago, I was faced with the same thing you are right now. I was a senior at Cory-Rawson High School. It was basketball season and my sixth and final year of playing ball. Even though I was in great shape, there was a big lump on the side of my neck. I didn't think anything about it because I was too healthy. I showed one of my coaches at school and he said I should get it checked out. That was the beginning.

My doctor said it could be leukemia, Hodgkin's or nothing at all.

After the necessary tests were run, I found out I had cancer. When they biopsied the lump on my neck, it was the size of an egg. It still didn't sink in. I was just concerned with what I was going to have to do. My doctors were worried because they thought it was all the way to my spleen.

I had loads of tests done, including two bone marrows. When I had my first bone marrow test, the doctor told me my bones were too strong from all the milk I drank regularly. So he had to do it twice! Yes, it was horrible and painful.

They set up my protocol for chemotherapy in March and said I would have at least six months of that. Happy senior year for me. I'm not going to lie to you. It was very hard and depressing at times. But it is a lot easier to have a good outlook when you know you will be healthy again in a year. Yet that's weird because I never felt sick in the first place.

I had my first chemo treatment the third week of March. I vomited eight times. I never wanted to go back. But the next week they gave me an anti-nausea drug and I didn't vomit after that. After two treatments, my attention was on losing my hair. I already had a beautiful wig and told myself I was ready to lose it and get it over with. But Kim, you can't get ready for something like that. It was really hard. All I can tell you is that it grows back and is even more beautiful than it was before. There is a plus about being bald. It doesn't take long to get ready for school! Hair is a small sacrifice when it comes to keeping your health and life. Don't forget that.

I kept going through my treatments. My doctor let me play in the All Star basketball game and I tried my best to keep busy. I didn't feel the best but I wanted to act like everything was all right. I did have six months of chemotherapy and then came radiation. That is a very intense treatment. My skin got burned but it treated a localized area. Radiation wasn't until September. Earlier that May, I graduated with my classmates. In the summer, I worked two jobs during the treatments. I didn't get to go to college until winter when they told me I was in remission! I am now starting my fourth year of remission. I will be graduating from Eastern Michigan University with a degree in sports medicine in April.

Kim, it was hell going through everything but today I am thankful because I have a perspective on life that few people our age have. You will get this perspective. I'm thankful for having a cancer that did not kill me, even though there were days I didn't want to live. There will be good days and bad days. Just believe!

Please call me if you need to talk or have any questions. I regret that I didn't have anyone to talk to. You're in my prayers, Kim.

Cheri McDougle

Change of Plans

Wednesday, November 1, 1995

My Aunt Juleen went with us today for my surgery. My great-aunt Marilyn lives near the hospital and was there to meet us when we arrived. It really does help to be surrounded by supportive family members. I know it helps Mom get through some of the long hours she has to spend in the waiting room.

I was introduced to the doctor who explained the procedure in detail. I was pretty much in terrifying disbelief when he used a roll of medical tape to represent the size of the port that was going to be inserted in my chest. He also put it under his scrubs to show how it would look under my clothes. Of course, he had to tell me about the chances of it becoming infected in the months ahead. If that were to happen, he would take it out and put another one in on the other side of my chest.

I went into panic mode and asked the nurse if she could get Mom. I had no idea the port would be so big. I prayed, "Lord, help me through this. I'm so confused. I don't want the doctor to get upset with me but I'm not ready for this. It just doesn't feel right."

God answered my prayer. When Mom got to my room, the nurse said there was a little boy in recovery who had his fourth port put in; she said she'd bring him by so that I could see what it looked like implanted under the skin. Once I saw this sweet blond-haired child who couldn't have been more than four years old, I felt so much sympathy and sadness for him. No child should ever have to suffer like this. When I saw the scars on his frail chest, I knew I didn't want an implanted port. When I shared this with the doctor, he said there was an alternative and he would be right back to show us another device. Once the doctor left, I will never forget what I said to Mom. It was a life-changing moment.

"I feel like God has been right here beside me, Mom. I really believe He sent the little boy to help me make the right decision. That little guy was like my angel boy. All this time I've been asking, "Why me, God?" Now I'm thinking, "Why not me, God?" I can feel the Holy Spirit working in me and making me stronger."

The doctor quickly returned to the room and showed us something called a Hickman catheter. He held up a white, thin tubular device and explained that it was a type of central venous catheter that would be inserted in my chest. He showed how one tube would enter through the jugular vein in my neck and it would then run through my body to the superior vena cava that is close to my heart. The rest of the catheter would come out of my chest, just above my right breast and two tubes (one light blue and one light green) would hang out.

Those tubes are where blood can be drawn and where the chemo drugs will be given. He stressed that the catheter would require flushing every other day with a drug called Heparin to prevent blood clots. Mom came through for me once again and assured the nurse that she could do this. Then the nurse spoke up and put me completely at ease when she said I could easily tuck the tubes in my bra. They would hardly be noticeable. I was sold completely when I heard that.

The doctor said my surgery went well and I have to admit that I'm really not in much pain. I keep staring at these two tubes sticking out of my chest. I'm going to follow Cheri's advice and try to keep a positive outlook. That's easy for me to say now because I don't have my first chemo treatment until Monday, November 6th. Who knows how I'll be feeling or what I'll be thinking by then?

I am feeling so thankful right now. My great-aunt Marilyn has insisted on buying me the best wig possible. She's such a blessing. We could buy a regular wig at a decent cost but we've been told that there is a company that makes wigs out of human hair. They look so real that you can wash, dry and style them like your own hair. Mom's beautician, Sandy, is helping us get things moving because I will probably be bald in a month. She's going to help my hair look as full as possible until it starts falling out in big clumps. She's going to take a sample of my hair and send it to the wig company for a close match in color. Sandy is another blessing. So many people are reaching out to help me and my family.

November Chemo

Sunday, November 5, 1995

My first chemo treatment is tomorrow. The plan is for Mom, Dad, Grandma Oglesbee and I to leave around 7 o'clock for an 8:30 appointment at the oncology clinic. I have no idea what time the chemo will start. I just know it will take a long time. I wonder if I'll be able to feel it running through my veins. My hands get cold and clammy every time I think about it. I've seen too many sad shows on TV where the person dies from cancer. Their eyes always look so hollow and their complexions are beyond pale. I'm reminded of the expression: 'If the cancer doesn't kill you, the chemo will.' Besides being bald, I wonder what I'll look like at the end of my treatments.

Mom and I had a really good talk this afternoon. For the first time since this horror began, I asked her to tell me what she's thinking and how she's managing to deal with everything I'm going through; she still continues to work and still keeps our family life as normal as possible. She's unbelievable. I'll never forget her telling me that she's praying she will be sick from my chemo and that I won't. What a testament to a mother's love!

She wants to wrap her arms around me every day and take away my fears and pain but she knows that she needs to step back at times and let me deal with things in my own way. I'm not someone who likes to be babied and I really appreciate how Mom and Dad are respecting that. I refuse to become "the girl with cancer." Whatever it takes, I'm going to be Kim. Mom believes I'll be a positive example for others one day. I hope she's right.

"Dear Lord, you know how scared I am. You know I'm afraid of dying. I'm trying to keep my faith and let you be totally in control. It's hard to do most of the time because I want to know right now if I'll really beat cancer. Lord, please give me the strength to survive the chemo and not get sick from all the side effects."

Monday, November 6, 1995

What a day! I can't believe I'm saying this but things went MUCH better than I expected. My 8:30 appointment with the oncologist went well. I liked her a lot. She examined my catheter and was very thorough in explaining the details of my treatment plan and the side effects I could experience. Her maternal instinct put me at ease when she prepped us with information for the rest of the day.

After a free lunch in the hospital cafeteria, I had to be admitted for an overnight stay. This was a precautionary measure the hospital required in case I had any adverse reactions to the chemotherapy.

I know I'm 16 years old and should probably be way past needing to hold stuffed animals for comfort but I've been given some by family and friends the past month that are special. So special that I've held them close night after night. I was so disappointed when I started unpacking my bag earlier tonight and realized I'd left them at home. Grandma came to my rescue and surprised me with a stuffed bear from the hospitality shop.

I packed a scarf to put on tomorrow in case my hair starts falling out immediately. I know this sounds paranoid; that's exactly what I am. According to my doctors and nurses, it won't start falling out for about three weeks but I'm not taking any chances.

The rest of the afternoon was pretty uneventful. I have to admit that it was pretty slick when the nurse hooked up my IV to the catheter. This was so much better than being poked with needles nonstop. My chemo treatment was scheduled to start at 6 o'clock. This seemed really late because the nurse said it would take between four and five hours. I know Mom and Grandma were trying especially hard to make small talk because they knew I was filled with sheer terror. As the chemo hour drew closer, Dad kept looking at his watch. Even though Mom wanted him and Grandma to head home before dark, there was no way he was going to leave until he saw with his own eyes that I could handle things.

My chemo began right on time. The nurse was really kind and asked me if I had any questions. If I did, I couldn't remember what they were because my lips were quivering so much. Once the chemo was released, I couldn't actually feel it. Instead, I envisioned it passing through every part of my body and killing every cell in its path. Chemo is relentless. It doesn't care which cells are good or bad. It attacks whatever it can with vengeance and no remorse. I picture it crawling methodically through my veins like a venomous spider intent on building intricate webs that will trap and destroy my immune system.

After Dad and Grandma left, Mom and I looked over the papers that described the chemo drugs I was given. I wasn't sure how to pronounce any of them. I know I'll forget their names eventually but will never forget the damage they'll probably do to my body. The common side effects from the Cytoxan are nausea/vomiting, loss of appetite, hair loss, low blood counts and a metallic taste in the mouth. Thankfully, they gave me a sucker that alleviated the metal taste. Common side effects of the Vincristine are constipation, jaw pain, hair loss, irritation of nerves, muscle weakness, and tingling of the fingers and toes. I'm holding out hope that I won't have many of these.

I was also started on some oral chemo drugs. The side effects from the Procarbazine include nausea/vomiting, diarrhea, low blood counts, flu-like symptoms, fatigue, fevers, chills, and muscle and joint aches. They also gave me Prednisone, a steroid that can increase the effectiveness of the anti-cancer meds I'm getting. Common side effects include increased appetite, weight gain, fluid retention, full or round 'moon' face, stomach upset, acne, muscle weakness, increased blood sugar and sugar in the urine, irritability, mood changes, less resistance to infection and longer time for healing.

WHEW! So it sounds like I'm in for it!

Tuesday, November 7, 1995

I didn't get much sleep last night. I know the nurses mean well but they came in to check on me so often. I'm sure Mom didn't sleep well either in her reclining chair. I'm having really bad cramps today and my stomach hurts constantly. But I haven't puked yet so that's good. Dad came back to the hospital this morning and we were able to leave around 12:30. I had a few friends come over tonight to visit. They wanted to see how I was doing. That brightened my day.

The first thing I did when I woke up this morning was check my pillow for any hair I might have lost during the night. So far so good. But the clock is ticking now that the chemo is in my body.

Wednesday, November 8, 1995

I went to school this morning around 10:30. Everyone was glad and surprised to see me. School went okay but I kept getting really hot and my stomach ached. I hope I can keep up with all my classes. If I feel as crappy as I did today, it's going to be a struggle.

Friday, November 10, 1995

Well, I had to make yet another trip to the doctor today. I was really dreading it because it was my first gynecologist appointment. Since Mom has worked for this doctor and the others on staff for years, she talked to them about options to preserve my ovaries in the hopes that I'll be able to have children one day. Even though I hate shots, I'm thankful for this drug called Lupron. I'll never stop believing that I can't get pregnant after I'm married. This seems like eons away.

So now I will get a shot each month that I'm on chemo. It will shut down my ovaries and my menstrual cycles and ovulation will stop. I'll be in a temporary stage of menopause. Yea! No periods for four months! I think the shot hurt worse than the actual exam. I guess I won't dread going back in the future. What's another shot when you've been prodded and poked as much as I have in one month. Mom will be able to give them to me. This eases my mind a lot. I was surprised to find out I've lost 10 pounds already.

Sunday, November 12, 1995

I felt a great peace at church today. We sang 'Our God is An Awesome God.' I love that song. It is so meaningful. During the praise and worship part of the service, our pastor asked me how my first week of treatments had gone.

So I stood up and addressed the congregation. I thanked them for their prayers and said my week had been okay. I told them about the stomach aches and how yesterday my throat started hurting and my fingers were tingly. I also confessed how scared I am about tomorrow because I go back for more IV chemo drugs.

Our pastor asked me if I'd like to come forward and be anointed with oil as he prayed for my healing. I didn't hesitate. I welcomed it. In scripture, oil was both a medicine and a symbol of the spirit of God. When the oil touched my forehead, I felt a warm penetration of peace.

What happened next was unforgettable. The pastor began talking about certain scriptures in the book of James. It was about praying for the sick. Every Sunday, we pray for those who have all kinds of physical and emotional concerns. I've seen others go down front to be anointed with oil but I never imagined experiencing it myself. As I bowed my head, my parents and sisters came forward to pray *for me. I could feel warm tears pooling in my eyes to know they were there beside me. Then the church elders came forward and so did many people in the congregation. I felt so loved. Prayer is becoming my safe haven.*

Monday, November 13, 1995

Mom's good friend, Linda, went with us to the oncology clinic today. Before starting my chemo, I had to go to the lab and get my blood count checked. That took forever! Finally, after being there three hours, I was prepped for the IV treatment. I saw the same doctor again and she was pleased that I got through this past week so well after the first chemo.

The chemo drugs today were Adriamycin, Bleomycin and Vinblastine. Adriamycin is a red liquid. Its side effects are nausea/vomiting, hair loss, urine may turn pink/red for 1-2 days after treatment, low blood counts and mouth sores. Side effects from the Bleomycin are low blood counts, darkening and peeling of the skin, dark rings in the nail beds, and scarring and stiffening of the lungs. I was already freaked out by the time I read about Vinblastine because it can cause low blood counts, constipation and abdominal pain.

Today did not go well. I hope this isn't a warning sign of things to come. By the time we got home, I felt absolutely miserable. My stomach hurts, I'm having hot and cold flashes and my head is throbbing. My throat is now very swollen and sore. I'm still taking the Zofran for nausea and hope this helps. I just want this all to stop!

Warm Jello

The day after the second chemo treatment, Jackie went to work after Kim insisted that she felt strong enough to stay home by herself. Everything changed by late morning. She became violently ill and barely had the strength to get from her bedroom to the bathroom. Her body shook from the brutal vomiting and diarrhea; every inch of her body screamed in pain as she dropped to the floor and cried out, "Just let me die!"

All the life had been ripped out of her. She sensed that death was swirling around her and waiting to proclaim victory. She was too sick to care. If a sharp knife had been within reach, she would have ended the earthly misery.

Several minutes passed before the room stopped spinning. Once Kim could feel her heartbeat slow down, she reached for the bathtub ledge to pull herself up to a sitting position. As much as she wanted to cry, she didn't. She feared it would lead to throwing up again. She sat still for a number of minutes and contemplated her next move. It seemed impossible; she was too weak. She was like a fragile bird with two broken wings.

She had to make a decision. She could sit there until her

mother got home from work or she could try to stand and walk on her own. On teetering legs, she made it to the sink. The mirror revealed the painful truth. She looked awful. Her hair was disheveled and her skin was morbidly pale. When she touched the dark and puffy circles under her eyes, she didn't recognize the stranger staring back at her.

As she slowly made her way back to the bedroom, the doorbell rang. While she had no intentions of opening the door and letting anyone see her, she was curious who would be stopping by at this time of day. She peered around the curtain and saw Brad's car in the driveway. He knew she was going to be home. They had talked on the phone the night before and he said he might stop by before going to work but she didn't think he'd actually do it.

Her heart surged with relief. She desperately needed someone to talk to at that very moment and felt comfortable knowing it was Brad. She opened the door without hesitation.

"Kim, I hope I didn't wake you up. I just wanted to stop and see how you're doing."

"No, I wasn't sleeping."

"How are things going today?"

"Not so good. I can't keep any food down. Mom always has us drink warm jello when we're sick. I was just trying to find the strength to make some. Come on in."

By the time they reached the kitchen, she didn't have the stamina to stand and crumpled to the floor.

"Don't even try to get up, Kim. That's an order."

Beyond telling him where to find the box of jello and a small pan, she was too exhausted to make conversation. He realized this and tried to lift her spirits.

"I've had warm jello before. When I was little, my grandma

made it for me if I was sick."

Within a few minutes, he poured the warm liquid in a coffee mug, sat on the floor and carefully handed it to her.

"Just sip it, okay? Make sure it isn't too hot."

"It's just right. It tastes good."

"But is it as good as your mom's?" he grinned.

"It's just as good. You know, we really could find a more comfortable place to sit."

Normally, Kim's independent spirit would have prevailed and she would have never asked for help. Brad knew all about her strong-willed personality and helped her up before she could object. For the next hour, they sat at each end of the couch and made small talk. He followed her lead in the conversation and didn't ask about the treatments. When it was time for him to leave, he said, "I need to head out. Just stay where you are. I'll check back to see how you're doing in a few days."

"Thanks for stopping, Brad. I'm sorry how terrible I look in my sweats and T-shirt. I can't believe I let anyone see me without makeup."

"Kim, I don't care about that. I care about you and how you feel."

Innocent Victim

Thursday, November 23, 1995

I'm very thankful for my life this Thanksgiving. I'm also thankful for prayer, God, the Bible, my mother, father, sisters, friends and family. I'm thankful for the way God has worked in my life already. I now have better priorities. There are times when I just want to give up and die. I know how but I'm thankful for my strong attitude and faith. I believe in prayers, healing and miracles. I know God's not finished with me yet.

One of my goals is to have just one person tell me they look up to me. Then I'll know I'm doing okay. I want people to see God through me because without Him, I would be nowhere. Everything has a purpose and God is in total control. I've learned so much more about peace, love, forgiveness, kindness, patience and acceptance. But most importantly, I've learned that worrying only makes things worse. It does no good. I've also noticed that it is often the little things around me that bring a smile to my face. They are the things I would have ignored at one time in my life but don't anymore. I thank God daily for my hair and I always will. I'm very thankful for those who accept me for me.

Saturday, November 25, 1995

I lounged around most of the day because I felt so terrible. I thought about telling Mom I didn't feel up to going to the Brinkman Thanksgiving supper but I wanted to see my relatives. I figured I'd perk up after my shower but that didn't happen.

After I put on my makeup, I started blow drying my hair. Without warning, large clumps landed in the sink. I felt like throwing up and thought this couldn't really be happening. I froze for a second. Then I panicked and yelled, "Mom, get in here! It's happening!"

She came right away and by then I'd lost more chunks. I pounded my fist on the sink in fear and anger. I knew I was going to lose it all right then. I know Mom was fighting back a lot of tears. She quickly started cleaning things up and dumping my hair in the wastebasket that was filled to the rim. She was trying to get it out of my sight as quickly as possible. I couldn't calm down until she held me.

"You aren't losing all your hair, Kim. It's just thinner in spots. Let me brush it gently to see if more falls out."

"When is my wig going to get here? If it all falls out before Monday, I can't go to school."

"I'll call Sandy again and have her check on it Monday morning. We can't get too far ahead of ourselves. Let me comb over the thin spots."

I have to admit that it looked a lot better than I thought it would when she was finished. Ever since I started chemo, I've wondered how long it would take to start losing my hair. Now I know the answer – just three weeks!

Only a Mother Knows

Jackie was extremely aware of Kim's health each day and learned there is never enough time to prepare for life-and-death hardships when it's your child facing them. God gave her that extra strength she needed when she ran into the bathroom and saw Kim's vibrant hair that lay lifeless in the sink. The entire time she was reassuring her that there were only a few thin spots, Jackie knew it was only going to be a few days until the thin areas would be bald.

Once Kim's panic attack ended and Jackie had the bathroom cleaned up, she checked on the other girls to make sure they were getting dressed. Then she slipped out of the house and headed to the shed to find Roger.

He was working on a tractor on the far side of the building when he heard the door close. He thought Jackie was coming to remind him that it was time to get ready for the party. Instead, he saw her leaning against the door. He knew immediately why she was sobbing. "It's started, Roger, and there's nothing we can do to make it go away."

When she showed him the wastebasket filled with hair, they held each other and cried. "Jackie, we are bigger than this attack on Kim and we'll fight this with all the strength we have until she is completely healed."

In Search of Identity

Monday, November 27, 1995

During homeroom, we watched a show on Channel 1 about a girl who had leukemia and went through chemo. I just about ran out of class crying. I lost a lot more hair this morning when I washed it. The wastebasket looked disgusting. I'm wondering how I'm going to tell people my hair is falling out. It's been nice this past weekend not having to take any chemo pills. I've felt free in a way. I'm still having bad headaches. My throat is sore and I have some pretty bad mouth sores that are making it difficult to eat.

Wednesday, November 29, 1995

I washed my hair this morning before school and a huge amount fell out. I didn't have time to cry or panic because I was more worried about getting to school on time. Mom called the administration and told them I'd be late. For the first time, you could see obvious bald spots. We pulled it all back in a clip and tried to hide them the best we could.

Mom had good news when I got home. My wig is in!

Thursday, November 30, 1995

Everybody at school is gullible or really good liars because they said they liked my hair. Maybe people were just trying to be nice. Natalie came over tonight and we washed and dried the wig to give it an even better look.

This wig issue is so crazy. I had a natural spot of gray hair before I lost it all and when the wig came in, the first thing Mom and I noticed were some strands of gray hair just like my real hair. We didn't specify that or anything. I think it's a God thing.

This has happened more than once. When Mom and I were on our way home from chemo one night, we joked how good a delicious dessert would taste but she was too tired to make anything. Shortly after we got home, there was a knock at the door. There stood Mom's dear friend, Cindy, with a plate of homemade apple dumplings that she knew we loved. This was another God thing.

More Than a Hairdresser

*J*ackie was anxious to call Sandy and thank her for everything she'd done. Soon after the wig arrived, she did just that.

"Hello."

"Sandy, it's Jackie. I had to call and tell you how grateful we are for everything you've done. The wig looks beautiful. It's so amazing that there are a few gray hairs in it that are just like Kim's natural hair and in the very same spot. I'll never forget that moment when Kim turned her head to look in the mirror and the light captured everything. We knew we had just witnessed another miracle of God's love for us, even in the smallest details."

"I thought the same thing when I first saw it, Jackie. I'm so pleased how nice it looks on her. I ran into one of Kim's teachers a few days ago and asked her how Kim looked in the wig. She said, "Kim doesn't have a wig." I told her she did but I don't think she believed me. I'm so relieved it came in just in time."

"I know I had to be driving you crazy when I kept calling and asking when it would get here. You were so patient, my friend."

"I would have done the same thing if it was my daughter. I'll always remember the day you said that you needed to leave this in the Lord's hands because He knew when she needed it. You were right. He knew best. The wig came the next day."

"Sandy, I know this has been difficult for you. Each time I've shed a tear watching Kim lose more hair, I know you've done the same."

"It was so hard not to break down and bawl when I was fitting her with her wig. I'll never forget that sick feeling when I started combing her hair and so much fell out that it filled the brown grocery bag beside the chair. None of us could hold back the tears. I could have put her hair in a ponytail and just pulled it out. I understand why she didn't want me to do it. I kept thinking, "She's only sixteen years old. She shouldn't have to be dealing with this.""

"I know. Thank you for everything. Words can't express how much we appreciate you."

"I adore Kim, Jackie. She's constantly in my prayers. You all are. I'll always be here if you need me for anything."

The Gifts

December 1, 1995

I found the lump two months ago today. It still doesn't seem real at times. I wore a hat to school for the first time. The baldness wasn't as noticeable because I still have a little bit of hair left. I actually felt comfortable wearing it compared to yesterday when I wore the wig. I think I've decided not to wear a hat all the time though. If I do, I will look like "the girl with cancer" everywhere I go. Everyone will see my bald head beneath the hat. But if I wear the wig, then hopefully I can just blend in and no one will notice. Maybe I can trick everyone who doesn't know me into believing that I'm healthy and cancer-free.

I'm still not satisfied with the wig. I need to make it look better so that no one will realize it's a wig. I've lost four more pounds. I've now lost 12 pounds since being diagnosed. I weigh 118. I had built some good muscle strength from lifting weights this past summer. Hope I'm not losing all of that.

December 3, 1995

I had the neatest surprise when I got home from Youth Group tonight. Dan Irwin brought me a beautiful picture frame. He told Mom that someone had given it to him last year when he was recovering from a very serious car accident that he was lucky to survive. I think everyone in our community wondered if Dan would ever be able to return to the Dan we all knew, a friendly and considerate guy who loved long distance running. After surgery and several months of grueling physical therapy, he was able to walk. People couldn't believe it when he started running again. It was so inspiring. He's a hero in my eyes.

The frame is brass with a light green mat. On the cream background in black lettering it says: 'Tough Times Never Last; Tough People Do.' He had received it as an inspirational gift from someone who had previously gone through a difficult time. He said he was passing it on to me because he felt like he was done with it and knew I was struggling with my treatments. He said to keep it as long as necessary and to draw strength from it. Then when I no longer need it, I should pass it on to someone else who is going through rough times.

I told Mom I want to put it somewhere in the house where it can be easily seen as a constant reminder that I'll get through this rough patch in my life. She's going to buy an easel and set it on the end table beside the couch in the living room. I really like this idea because my family will see it often, too. It's a reminder for me to let my parents and sisters know how much I appreciate them; my cancer is as hard on them as it is on me.

A piece of paper is taped to the back of the frame with these names in order: Joyce Schroeder, Dan Irwin, Kim Brinkman. I don't know who Joyce Schroeder is but I'm going to find out. I'm so touched that Dan chose to give this to me. It's come at a time when I really need it. I'm feeling worse each day and still have a lot more chemotherapy to go.

December 7, 1995

Yesterday's chemo took over five hours. Even though I have stomach cramps, hot flashes and feel extremely tired, I made myself go to school today. I can't sleep at night because the hot flashes wake me up every 1-2 hours. I would have rather stayed home but I don't want to miss more school. I wonder if my teachers and friends see through my facade; I'm trying so hard to appear that I can handle everything. Truthfully, it takes all of what little energy I have to even get dressed in the morning. I'm like that clown at the circus who looks happy with the painted smile but is crying on the inside.

December 10, 1995

I'm writing this entry in a new journal I got tonight. Mom and Dad gave it to me when they got home from her office party. Mom hadn't even planned on going because she had already committed to singing in a church Christmas cantata in town. When she told her co-workers this, they insisted that Mom and Dad at least come to the meal. So they did.

When they got ready to leave, Mom's close friend, Shirley, said,

"Wait just a minute before you go. We have some gifts for you to take to Kim. We hope this will brighten her days while she's undergoing treatment."

I don't even know where to begin in describing what the doctors and the co-workers did for me. It had to be very emotional for Mom when they brought out a decorated box filled with balloons and all kinds of wrapped presents with numbers on them. There was also a small Christmas tree with numbers on the branches that were attached with wrapped presents. There were so many gifts that I could open one every other day until my treatments were finished. It was so unbelievable!

There were beautiful gifts from people I didn't even know, including patients who heard about my cancer. I even got gifts from people at the hospital who had performed some of my tests. This means so much to me that people went out of their way to make me feel special.

I let each of my sisters open a gift for me tonight. I wanted them to feel included because they were as excited as I was. By the time we were done, I had this new journal, a stuffed animal, bookmarks, makeup, potpourri, jewelry and an angel pin. I am so thankful to everyone who made this happen. I wish I knew all their names and addresses so that I could write them personal notes of gratitude.

I looked at Mom and said, "I can't believe people did all this for me. I wonder why, especially when some of them don't even know me?" Mom smiled and said, "These are gifts of love, Kim."

December 13, 1995

Tara went with Mom and me to my chemo appointment today. It was nice for a friend to be there and see what actually goes on. Unfortunately, today's treatment was the bad one with the red liquid. This medicine is like a poisonous elixir that is bent on nearly killing me at times.

I didn't let on to Tara how much I feared it would make me sick but after we stopped at Arby's on the way home, it was obvious. My throat started to swell and my stomach hurt. These symptoms were ones I know all too well. The red liquid means I won't be able to go to school tomorrow. I'll be spending most of the day in the bathroom with diarrhea and vomiting... and that's putting it mildly.

I feel like a teenage girl who is trapped in the body of an unhealthy 50-year-old woman. I feel so out of control. I can't concentrate in school because the hot flashes are getting worse. Mom says it's because the Lupron shots make my body think I'm in menopause. There are times when I'm so nauseated that I can't stand the thought of food. Then there are times when I'm so hungry I want to eat and eat but I don't want to gain back the weight I've lost. I guess I like being this weight right now. So I have an internal struggle of whether to eat when I'm hungry or not.

I read somewhere that people go through five stages of grieving when they lose someone they love. I feel so sick tonight that I'm grieving for my own body. I'm grieving that I'm no longer who I once was. There are times when I just want to go to bed and sleep forever ... and I really mean forever. Then there are times when I'm afraid of dying in my sleep.

December 20, 1995

I've received a lot of thoughtful Christmas cards from relatives, friends and people at church. I'm thankful for all of them but the card I received today holds extra special meaning. It's one I will treasure all my life.

On the front is a picture of a cute dog with a stethoscope around his neck and a doctor's bag beside him. He's pointing at another cute dog that has a very red nose and doesn't feel well from the look in his eyes. When you open the card, it says: HEAL!

This is the handwritten message that was inside:

Dear Kim,

I've been thinking a lot about you lately. I have pretty good grapevine sources from several people who care a great deal for you and your family. So I hear quite a bit.

I have several prayer groups praying for you to get completely better and I have faith that it will happen. I got the feeling from seeing you in the office that you and your family have a calm strength that usually comes from a great Christian faith. You and your mom portray a "we can handle this" attitude that I rarely see in people. I really appreciate knowing you and I wish you a great Christmas and a great future.

Sincerely,
Dr. Robertson

That Fine Line

As Kim's body deteriorated, the bleak months of January and February dampened her spirits more. The red liquid was on a rampage and in total control. The mouth sores multiplied and she felt worse with each passing day. The intense headaches and hot flashes were constant. She began having sharp pains in her chest while her lungs felt heavy at times and ached. Her dry skin was visibly scaly and her brittle fingernails began to peel. The volatile mood swings intensified with the self-imposed pressure of maintaining good grades and going to school when she felt so ill.

She had lost so much weight that it was difficult for Jackie to find even a hint of muscle where the Lupron could be injected. Once she started to feel the needle hitting Kim's hip bone, Jackie couldn't handle giving her more injections. That's when she asked for help. Between her sister-in-law, Pam, who was a nurse and her colleagues at work, Kim received the injections she needed.

January 8, 1996

I went for my third chemo treatment today and felt more nervous than usual. I know Mom is just as nervous. I already feel so sick all the time that I wonder how much more my body can take.

Before the treatment, I followed the same routine. I had a urine test, got weighed and had blood work done to check my white blood cell count. It's always in the back of my mind that my count might be too low and then the chemo treatment would be cancelled until I was stronger. So far that hasn't happened but I wonder when my luck is going to run out.

I felt so uneasy when one of the doctors examined all of the areas where the lymph nodes are. I was really ticked when he told me to take off my hat in front of him. That bothered me so much. How rude! It's bad enough that I'm losing my eyelashes and eyebrows. Why did he need to see my bald head?

When I told him I was short of breath, he ordered a pulmonary function test to see if and what kind of damage the chemo was doing to my lungs. Lung damage is one more side effect and they told me I might easily get short of breath the rest of my life.

One of my friends told me I looked too skinny the other day. I know she means well and cares about me. She wants me to look healthy. Is this what others think about me too? I guess I try to make myself think I'm healthy when I exercise from time to time by running, lifting weights, and doing sit-ups and push-ups. But I'm not healthy. It's so depressing. I feel like I'm falling apart emotionally and physically. When I feel so crappy on my non-chemo days, I wonder if I am dying of cancer.

One night as Kim was getting ready for bed, she noticed some dark brown stripes on her skin that were exactly where her clothes had touched her body that day. Even though she remembered that this was a possible side effect from the chemo, she was scared and wanted her mother to see them.

When Jackie walked into the bedroom, Kim was in the process of getting undressed. While Jackie immediately noticed the marks, she was more taken aback when she saw the skin that was barely clinging to the visible ribs on Kim's naked body. Jackie was speechless with concern.

"Mom, I know these marks are one of the side effects of chemo but do you think they'll ever go away?"

"We'll talk to the doctor about this, honey. Your next appointment is in a few days. Do you still have so many mouth sores?"

"Yes. They're so bad it hurts to eat anything. The medicine doesn't help."

"We're going to talk to the doctor about this too. I'll make some mild soups that won't irritate things more. We need to get you on a supplemental drink that is filled with nutrients and calories your body needs."

"You don't have to hide what you're thinking, Mom. I can tell I'm losing too much weight. I know you're wondering if I'm starting to be anorexic. I've wondered the same thing lately. There are times when I just don't have an appetite. Then there are times when I eat and feel like a pig. Is it bad that I kind of like it that my pants feel loose and baggy?"

"Honey, I have been worried. You and your sisters are all beautiful girls with slender figures. I don't want any of you to ever go on a diet. You're all perfect just the way you are. And you, my dear, are a smart girl. You know you need to eat for your body to continue healing."

"I know where that fine line is. I'll do my best not to lose more weight. Even when I don't feel like it, I'll try to eat."

"Thank you. That's all I can ask."

"Now don't get mad but I'm wondering if you've ever read my journal. I've written some pretty private things. Tell me the truth."

"I've never lied to you, Kim, and I'm not going to start now. I've never read your journal; there have been moments when I've wondered what you've been writing but I would never cross that line and violate your privacy. I have so much faith in you. If there's something you think I need to know for your own well-being, I know you'll tell me."

"I don't think I've written anything that would surprise you. Even though I've become more guarded lately with my feelings, it still seems like you know what's going on inside me. You do know, don't you?"

"Give me a hug and I'll tell you how I know. The moment you were born, I held you close to my chest and felt the miracle of your heartbeat. I feel that same joy now. I can feel your heart beating at the same rhythm as mine. They're beating as one. I think God gives this gift to mothers - an instinct for what our children are feeling."

"I hope God gives me this gift one day."

"I'm praying for it, honey."

Surrender

February 5, 1996

I'm so tired. I've felt very lonely all week and have longed for someone to talk to and share my feelings. I'm sure it has something to do with my final chemo treatment that's coming up at the clinic. I did get my prom dress. It's long and black. I'm looking forward to wearing it. But what about having a date?

February 17, 1996

Wouldn't you know that I'd come down with a cold the week of my very last chemo. My head feels like it's going to explode from the pressure and I'm coughing constantly. I tried taking some over-the-counter medication last night but had a terrible reaction. I got dizzy, had ringing in my ears and trouble hearing.

I was scared when we got to the hospital; I had this sinking feeling that my white blood cell count would be too low. I was so surprised and relieved when they said my numbers were within range and I could have the treatment.

This was the horrible, ravaging chemo. It was bad enough with the nonstop puking and diarrhea I had for several days; having a terrible cold on top of it was just too much. I spent most of the week in bed. When my head was still throbbing by Friday, Mom called the doctor's office and told them how awful I felt. They wanted to see me as soon as possible. After the doctor examined me, I was admitted to the hospital. My white blood cell count had taken a bad dive and so had my weight. I was too sick to even care.

By the next morning, my blood cell count had dropped again. I was put on an antibiotic and had to have a blood transfusion that took four hours. I had a lot of time to think. I told God if this was the time for Him to take me, then it was okay with me. I felt so miserable that I wanted to surrender.

Once I made it through the weekend in the hospital, I started to feel better. This was a turning point in my life. I realized that God still has a mission here on earth that He wants me to carry out. It isn't my time to go to heaven yet.

The Birthday

March 20, 1996

Today is my birthday. I've let so much time lapse in keeping up with my journal. I'm just trying to keep up with my daily life. Mom fixed lasagna for supper. This and the birthday cake tasted better than I can ever remember. When I blew out the candles, I silently wished: "I hope my seventeenth year of life goes better than my sixteenth year did."

A few days ago, I received the best early birthday present imaginable when the doctor said, "Kim, your scans have all come back negative."

Seconds after spontaneous tears of relief slid down my cheeks and Mom's, the doctor told me my name had been pulled to receive radiation treatments as part of the clinical protocol. I suddenly had mixed feelings. Part of me said, "No, I don't want more treatments of any kind. I'm in remission and free of cancer. I just want to move on with my life. My body needs to be left alone." The other part of me said, "Radiation is only for a short period of time and it won't be painful. Maybe this is a sign from God that I'll feel a little more secure in knowing I'll have it as an extra precaution. Then I'll know I've done everything possible to beat the merciless enemy."

While I've chosen to ignore so many frightening statistics since my diagnosis, I'll always remember that very day when the doctor put my life in sobering perspective. "Kim, you'll need to have routine check-ups and blood work done every three months. At the end of the year, we'll need to repeat your body scans again. If everything goes well, the check-ups and scans will be spaced out during the next five years. If you have a clean bill of health after five years, you can consider yourself cured."

When Mom and I left the office, I couldn't wait to get to the car. I needed to pray. Mom did too. So I prayed for both of us. "WOW, dear Lord! Thank you so much for the good results of all my scans. Thank you for my healing! You know that I really want to skip the 12 radiation treatments and move on. Yet I understand that you know what is best. I continue to trust in your plans for my life. I know you'll be with me and I am so thankful. Amen."

Making the Effort

April 15, 1996

I had a great time with my friends at prom! I danced until I was exhausted. It never entered my mind that I was a cancer victim. It was exhilarating to feel normal. When I found the lump in the fall, I didn't know how many weeks or months I might live. I didn't know if I'd even make it to enjoy a high school prom. How could I not have danced the night away in delirious joy? Even though I'm diagnosed for the moment as being 'cancer free,' I must admit that I'm always wondering. Am I truly rid of it forever? What if they missed something?

I'm glad I'm in the musical with my friends. Some nights I'm really too tired to go to practice, especially after working out for track. I'm really pushing myself but it's worth it; I feel like I belong again. Even though I know that I'm not even close to being in physical shape to fully participate in track, the coaches are letting me do what I can.

It's been a long time since I've written in my journal because I'm already done with the radiation treatments that targeted my chest and neck. Since the treatments were at Blanchard Valley Hospital, I was able to have them and still make it back in time for track.

I had a cradle or mold that was made for my body size. I had to lie in this hardened foam and the technician lined me up with the necessary areas of my body that received the radiation beams. It often took longer to be lined up correctly on the table than it did to receive the actual treatments.

When I was in the early stages of being prepared for radiation, I was given four permanent ink tattoos on my chest - one on each side of my chest and two on the front. These were markers that determined if my body was lined up properly.

I couldn't help but think of my dad and my rebellious nature. I've always wanted to get a tattoo in high school but he said, "None of my daughters will get a tattoo while living under my roof!" It's humorous that part of God's plan for my life is to have tattoos in spite of my dad's rules. I look forward to teasing him about this for a very long time.

I knew when my cancer treatments started that there was a chance my heart and lungs could be damaged. When my final medical report came back, it said there was 10% lung damage and very minimal heart damage. I guess that isn't too bad in the big scheme of things.

Mixed Emotions

By late April, Kim's side effects from the chemo and radiation were slowly diminishing. She continued to have the headaches that weren't quite as severe, although the nausea and vomiting still occurred with little warning. In spite of all this and the radiation treatments that tired her further, she received all A's and B's on her report card.

In her concerted efforts to appear as healthy and normal as her classmates, Kim looked forward to the trip to Quebec, Canada, with the French class. She was certain she was physically strong enough to go. Jackie and Roger were skeptical; they questioned whether her weak immune system could handle the rigors of traveling.

Jackie voiced these concerns to the school administrators who were comfortable in Kim making the trip because two of the chaperones were nurses. Upon learning that her sister-in-law, Pam, was one of the chaperones, Jackie's fears subsided. Pam knew everything about Kim's health situation and had the medical training to deal with any unforeseen problems.

Even so, it was bittersweet watching Kim board the bus. "She looked so skinny and frail today, Roger. I know her friends and the chaperones are looking out for her. I'm going to focus on her huge smile when she waved goodbye to us. It's hard to accept but she needs to be on her own; she needs to be away from us and everything that's a reminder of the past eight months of her life. She needs to be with her friends."

"She'll do fine, Jackie. God has her back."

The Race

April 30, 1996

I ran the 100 yard dash today in the first and last race of my junior year. The track meet was at Bluffton College; it was so cold and that made me even more nervous. I can't say enough about the encouragement from my teammates and coaches who looked out for me during practices and ran beside me if I seemed short of breath.

When I stepped up to the starters' line, it was hard to hear the gun sound because there was this reverberating cheer for me from a huge crowd of people standing near the finish line. It was AWESOME seeing all my family, teammates, friends, and tons of other people who had come to support me.

My prayer from the beginning was to finish without collapsing. I just wanted to finish the race. Mom told me later that she kept praying my ball cap didn't fly off. Both of our prayers were answered. Even though I came in last, I feel like I won the race! While I was trying to catch my breath, my family and friends were all hugging me and crying. I'm glad Dad caught everything on tape; it will be a life-

time reminder of this special moment. I hope my determination to never give up was an inspiration to others, especially those going through cancer. I didn't have the physical strength to run this race alone. God carried me across the finish line. I could feel it.

The Interview

Thursday, May 2, 1996

I just had an interview with a reporter who writes for our town newspaper. I wasn't nervous at all when he asked several questions. It didn't bother me when he took the picture of me wearing my ball cap either.

I really tried to stress how being diagnosed with cancer has given me a new perspective on life and how my priorities have changed; I've learned to appreciate my family and friends so much more. I said, "My family is probably my best friend now. Without them, my friends, and my strong belief in God, I don't know how I could have gotten through everything."

I told the reporter I'd like to write a book someday about everything I've gone through. Surviving cancer has also encouraged me to consider a career in the medical field where I could work with children. I want my life to be a witness to others of God's grace.

Another Hero

May 20, 1996

Ever since Dan Irwin gave me the inspirational plaque, I've wondered who Joyce Schroeder was and the part she played in my receiving it from Dan. I got my answer today and feel even more blessed. I received this letter from Kelli, one of Joyce's daughters.

Dear Kim,

After reading the inspirational article about you in the newspaper recently, I was once again touched by your courage and determination to make the most of your life. I would like to share with you a little bit about the original 'possessor' of the 'Tough Times Never Last; Tough People Do' plaque. My mom, Joyce Schroeder, was given this saying from my oldest sister, Deanna.

In September of 1988, Mom was diagnosed with breast cancer and until September 22, 1992, she fought extremely hard for her life. She traveled a similar path as you that included months of chemotherapy. While fighting back tears, I vividly remember shaving the strings of hair from her balding head and I truly felt the hurt of her losing her beautiful, thick hair.

She and my dad even traveled to Europe for several weeks. However, in the fall of 1991, we found out that the cancer had spread to her bones and liver. Our options were simply to do nothing with little time left for her, undergo more chemo that could give her possibly several months more, or have a bone marrow transplant with time left unknowing. Mom chose the transplant.

So in October of 1991, she went to the Cleveland Clinic for close to a month where they drained her marrow, cleaned it, and gave it back to her for new life. She was never sicker than during that time period but she made it through. Because of her strength and fighting spirit, she lived close to another year.

In that year, she went on a Caribbean cruise with my older sister, Bonnie. She and my dad also walked me down the aisle when I married my husband, Mark, on May 5, 1992. She celebrated with my younger sister, Kristi, when she was accepted into medical school and enjoyed being surprised with a party for her 50th birthday in August with all of her family and dearest friends. We said our last goodbyes to her in September.

I've shared with you the struggles of her cancer but leaving the cancer behind, I'd like to tell you a little bit about her: the 'cancer-free' person. Obviously, she was a strong person to fight such a battle but she was more than that. She was extremely caring of others, very hard working, fun, and as our priest called her, "the giggle of life." She could brighten a dull moment and make the best of any situation. She was in the highest of rankings when it came to motherhood.

She had a smile that helped others carry on. She was the best hugger ever. I can honestly say that when I think about it, I can still physically feel her hug me. Above all, she was devoted to God. She had such a strong faith and no matter what life dealt her, the Lord was in her. Because of her love for our Heavenly Father, I find strength now in knowing that she could never be happier than she is now.

The 'Tough Times Never Last; Tough People Do' saying was/is a meaningful quote for my mom and our entire family. There are little incidences that often happen which remind my dad, my three sisters, my brother and I that Mom continues to spread her love to others here. Reading about your courage, your recovery, and your faith in the Lord have helped our family; so thank you.

I truly believe that God puts people on earth for a mission and then when He chooses, they continue their duties in heaven. You have encouraged our family by passing on those powerful words of 'Tough Times Never Last; Tough People Do' to so many others. I am sure that my mom would thank you, and as I said, she is one of the best huggers; so if you think about it, she's probably sending one your way!

May God bless you and continue to strengthen you in a complete recovery. All my best to you and your entire family.

Kelli Roney

Uncertain

August 25th, 1996

Tomorrow is the first day of my senior year. My hair has grown back and I like the short haircut style I'll have for my senior pictures. I have to admit that I never thought my hair would look this good again. I'm getting so many compliments.

I'm glad the summer months are behind me. There was so much conflict, especially with my emotions and resenting the rules my parents are still enforcing. You'd think they could give me more freedom by now.

September 2, 1996

Mom told me today that she and Dad are aware how often Brad and I are talking on the phone. I hate feeling like I'm being backed into a corner, so I didn't say anything in response. Then she told me if I planned on dating him, they wanted to get to know him. She made it perfectly clear that he needed to see us together as a family and to join in our activities. She also said they were concerned about a rumor they'd heard that he was really into the partying scene.

So then I was ticked and started walking away. I didn't get too far until she said, "Do not walk away from me when I'm talking to you, young lady! You ARE going to bring him home." Then I made the mistake of saying, "Okay! Fine! I'll think about it!"

I should have kept my mouth shut because Dad raised his voice and said, "There is no thinking about it, Kim. If you plan on seeing Brad, we're going to get to know him. That's the way it is, whether you like it or not."

Brad is so easy-going that I know he'd be fine spending time with my family. I'm the one who would be nervous. I don't know when we went from being good friends to having strong feelings for one another but it's happened. I'm so confused. I don't want him to see someone else but I still want to be able to do things with other guys. I know this is immature on my part and unfair. I can't have it both ways even though that's what I want right now.

It sounds shallow but part of me wants to mold him into the person I know he can be. Although I'll never tell anyone this, I can actually picture us getting married. This would shock my family and some of my friends who are questioning why I'm even dating him. I know my parents aren't crazy about him but they really don't know him. I know he'd walk away from the wild lifestyle he's living to be with me. I'm the only one who realizes it.

He's so serious and has said more than once he loves me. I know he means it. I care about him so much but I keep second-guessing our relationship. What if he cheats on me? What if he betrays the trust I have in him? For all I know, he might be asking the same questions about me. We need to talk about all this at some point but I'm just not ready. When Mom and Dad set me straight tonight, it was all I could do to keep from admitting that I'm attracted to Brad's wild side. Part of me is drawn to this type of guy.

Senior Year

September 9, 1996

I got some good news today. My chest x-ray came back clear and my white blood cell count is very good. The doctor did a thorough exam of my lymph nodes and there are no problems. Thank you, God.

I just found out that the student body voted for me to be the herald in the Homecoming Court which really surprised me. I'm looking forward to the dance and getting caught up in all the excitement leading up to it. I can't help but think what my life was like a year ago at this time.

School is going so slowly. I'm thankful for my job at 'The Granary Gift and Furniture Barn.' Dianne and Steve Schafer own it and I don't know where you'd find nicer people. I'm working Monday nights and Saturdays. I absolutely love it. I wish this could be my full-time job after graduation and forget about going to college but Mom and Dad are insisting on a college degree. I'm checking out two schools that offer degrees in massage therapy. I'm not real excited about it.

October of 1996

I'm so happy with the way my senior pictures turned out. I've gotten a lot of compliments from family members and friends. The biggest surprise was receiving an advertising brochure in the mail the other day from the photographer. It's filled with pictures from seniors throughout the county and the photographer used one of my poses for the front cover.

I keep thinking about Brad. He's moved into a house with some other guys. I'm not too sure about this. It will mean more partying. That's the last thing my parents need to hear! The more I try to get him out of my mind, the more I think about him. I wish I could say I trust him completely but I'm not there yet. If I have the opportunity to date other guys this year, I will. Maybe then I'd know how I really feel about him - if he is really more than my comfort guy who is always there to listen.

My friends and I can't wait for graduation. I wish it was tomorrow. I want to be one of the four class speakers that day. I know there are other kids who also want to do this. We'll have to write a graduation speech and give it in front of a group of the teachers. Then they'll decide who will speak. I'm definitely going to include some of the things I went through last year and thank so many people who helped me and my family get through everything. My eyes are starting to water just thinking about it.

Decisions

Two more weeks until I graduate!

I can't believe that I've practically let my entire senior year go by without writing in my journal. I couldn't have had a better time with my friends and I feel at ease with some decisions I've made about my future.

Brad and I started dating several months ago. That's when he began joining in with our family activities. He feels comfortable with everyone; Mom and Dad appreciate how respectful and personable he is. They liked him immediately. I knew they would. For the most part, things have gone well in our relationship. There have been a few times when he's disappointed me by cancelling our plans to do things with his buddies.

I've decided to enroll in the massage therapy program that isn't nearly as far away as the other one I was considering. My classes will be every Saturday for one year; there will be an intense amount of work. I'll be able to save money by living at home and I'm going to ask Dianne if I can pick up more hours at work.

I don't want to be away from Brad. I don't want a long distance relationship that could jeopardize our future together. Even though we haven't talked about it, I know in my heart that he feels the same way.

Graduation Day

*T*he gymnasium was filled to capacity for the graduation ceremony. Families and friends were armed with cameras and extra batteries to capture the poignant memories. As the processional began, proud parents looked at one another and sighed; time had passed too quickly in their children's lives.

Kim was sitting in the front row beside her other classmates who were also receiving honor diplomas for their excellent academic achievements. When it was her turn to deliver the speech that she had worked on for days, she walked to the microphone with impeccable poise. Her smile was radiant and her dark hair picturesque. A particular hush resonated throughout the audience when she shared these feelings that many would never forget.

"Tough times never last; Tough people do. We, the graduating seniors of Columbus Grove are examples of some of these tough people. Think now of all the tough circumstances you've encountered. Each and every one of us has faced events we found tough to handle or thought would never end. As for those of us on this platform, we made it past the scary yet exciting first day of kindergarten. We've gone through all the pain from our loose

teeth throughout our grade school years and those terrible bumps, bruises, and scrapes that seemed to last forever. But those times didn't last. We did.

Then came junior high. At some point, we all seemed to somehow get in trouble. There were those weekend groundings we found so embarrassing that we thought would never be over, the relationship break-ups that we thought we'd never get over and the constant on-again and off-again friendships. Now those events seem so minor but then we felt like there would be no tomorrow.

High school has brought many more tough times. There were harder practices and more break-ups. We've had to work hard to make the grades and some have also had jobs or sports to contend with. We've lived for the weekends, only to barely be able to drag ourselves out of bed on Monday morning.

The fact that we are here today shows that we've survived these circumstances. We never gave up. As we journey into the future, many more tough times are bound to come our way and we will be faced with many new decisions and possibly life-changing events. As teenagers, we never think that anything bad will come our way. We choose to live life to its fullest with no responsibilities and our only decisions are where the next party is and if we will be there. But last year my family and I went down one of the toughest roads that anyone will ever walk.

One day I'm living life to its fullest and the next day I'm being diagnosed with cancer. Knowing that I could die made me do a lot of soul-searching and changing my priorities. It was during this time that I was given a framed quote from Dan Irwin that had been given to him when he was facing a tough time in his life.

I drew inspiration from this during the four months of chemotherapy and twelve sessions of radiation I endured. It would *have been so easy for me to give up when I was going through those painful days but I wanted to be a cancer survivor. Facing these classmates daily last year pushed me to survive. They offered kind words, gifts, prayers, and memories that I will never forget. They always accepted me - sick, weak and bald. They pulled together to show that they would never give up on me. For this, I thank you classmates, from the bottom of my heart. You, my family, friends and God are the reasons I'm alive to graduate with you tonight.*

I wish happiness and luck to my classmates with the road ahead they must travel. And I hope in times of trouble, they remember these seven wonderful words of encouragement: "Tough times never last; Tough people do!"

When the ceremony ended and the graduates walked into the hall, Kelli Roney was standing there to introduce herself to Kim. She shared how touched she was by the speech and thanked her repeatedly. Kim responded by saying how much she appreciated Kelli's letter and learning about her mother's courageous life.

Before she knew it, Kim was swarmed with hugs from her family and friends. People from her church and the community made a point to congratulate her on the powerful speech. One such person who was extremely moved by her words was Dan Irwin.

Then she saw Brad standing in the background; he held out his arms and she couldn't get to him fast enough. She buried herself in the embrace and savored his words. "Kim, I'm so proud of you. You can conquer anything."

She kissed him softly on the cheek. "I wanted you to be proud of me. I hope you could hear me thanking you during the speech. You're the one who always made me smile. You still do."

Family Time

The summer months passed quickly and Kim and Brad spent every possible minute together when they weren't working. She especially enjoyed getting to know Brad's mother, Mary, his step-dad, Russell, and his brothers, Josh and Justin. She also learned first-hand that Brad wasn't exaggerating when he praised his Uncle Larry's cooking skills. She had never eaten more delicious homemade noodles in her life.

It was also during those summer months that Brad made two crucial decisions. He moved back home and concentrated on saving money; he was ready to walk away from the care-free lifestyle he'd been living. This was a turning point in his life as well as Kim's. Any trust issues she might have harbored were gone; she was ready to relinquish her heart to him completely.

Although he didn't realize it at the time, his second decision was life-changing. While Kim had been raised going to church every Sunday her entire life, Brad's experience had been limited to being in Sunday school as a young boy. Even though they had never talked in depth about the vast difference in their religious backgrounds, they knew it was an issue that would need to be discussed at some point.

One Saturday night he casually mentioned to Kim that he'd meet her at church the next morning. She was startled. "Brad, that would be so nice. Are you sure? I hope you aren't feeling any pressure from me because I would never do that."

"No, there's no pressure. It's something I want to do." He kissed her goodnight and said with a smile, "Don't forget to save me a seat."

Before leaving for church that next morning, Kim told Jackie what Brad had said. She was as pleasantly caught off-guard as Kim had been. "Is this something the two of you have been talking about lately?"

"Not really. I've never wanted him to feel like he has to be in church to please me. It needs to be his decision. I don't know if he'll show up or not." These were Jackie's same thoughts that she kept to herself.

Minutes before the service began, Brad walked in and quickly spotted Kim and her family. He sat down beside her and whispered, "Are you surprised I made it?" She nudged his arm and smiled. "I'm just glad you're here. I was hoping I didn't save you a seat for nothing."

Jackie looked at Roger and smiled.

Grandma Mary

When Kim started classes at massage therapy school in the fall, she quickly realized how rigorous and time-consuming it would be for the next 12 months. In addition to keeping up with school work, she was putting in a lot more hours at The Granary throughout the week. She loved every aspect of her job and was delighted when presented with the opportunity to take on some of the office responsibilities. By now, she and Brad were on the same mission: to work hard and save money towards their future. They yearned to be together and had the days counted until Kim was finished with school. The search for the perfect engagement ring was well underway.

Whenever Brad had a day off from work, he stopped to see his Grandma Mary who virtually raised him while his mother worked. Even though her health was in noticeable decline, her spirits were lifted the minute he walked in the door and shared what his week had been like. Inevitably, they would talk about Kim. Then she would remind her grandson how happy she was that he had found such a wonderful girl.

Brad's beloved Grandma died in June. He was devastated to

have lost the woman who taught him the value of hard work and honesty. Kim was by his side to catch the tears and to help him through the grieving. In witnessing his compassionate soul, she loved him even more.

The Shed

*B*rad was in the kitchen talking to his mother and Uncle Larry when the phone rang that Saturday morning. The man who was calling worked at the jewelry store where Kim and Brad had been looking at engagement rings. He explained that one of the rings they looked at was being discontinued. If Brad was still interested, he would need to purchase it rather quickly or put some money down on it.

Brad was more than interested. He wanted that very ring. Kim had picked out two rings she especially liked but wanted Brad to surprise her with his final decision. He told the salesman to hold the ring and that he would pick it up that very day. As soon as he hung up the phone, he looked at the clock to see if he could make it to the bank in time to withdraw money from his savings account. Having heard the phone conversation, Brad's Uncle Larry said, "I can loan you some money for the ring." Brad was already headed out the door. "I've got the money. I just need to get to the bank before it closes."

With money in hand, Brad purchased the beautiful engagement ring that he thought Kim would especially like. The minute he walked out of the store, he headed home to show his mother the token of love he'd purchased. Mary was so touched when he showed it to her and said more than once, "Kim is a darling girl, Brad. She is so good for you." When she asked when he planned to propose, he quickly said, "I've got to call Jackie and Roger first. I need to ask their permission to marry Kim. I'm going to call right now because she's still at school."

Roger was working in the shed when the phone rang. "Roger, this is Brad. I was wondering if I could stop by in a few minutes and talk to you and Jackie before Kim gets home."

"Come on over. Jackie's in the house but I'll call her on the intercom. Just come out to the shed."

Even though it was less than a five-minute drive to their house, Brad was so nervous that it felt like he'd never get there. When he walked into the shed, Jackie and Roger were there to greet him. He did his best to disguise how nervous he was but it was to no avail. Jackie sensed this immediately and tried to ease his anxiety. She knew in her heart why he had come.

"We always enjoy seeing you, Brad. Is everything okay?"

"Sure. Everything's okay. I've come to ask your permission to marry Kim."

Jackie thought she was prepared for this moment but she wasn't. She looked at Roger for help but realized he couldn't find the words either. It was up to her to carry on the conversation.

"Brad, we couldn't love you more than we do. Thank you for being such a gentleman to ask our permission. Kim is our firstborn daughter and we're probably extra protective for that reason. We've prayed since her birth that she would one day find a man who would treat her with the love and respect she deserves. We've prayed for a young man who would commit his life to Christ and raise his children in a godly home. We know you're that young man in our hearts but there are a few things we need to share before giving our consent. We need to be sure that you realize Kim's cancer could return at some point and that she may never be able to have children. Have you thought about this?"

"Kim and I have talked about all this. I love her so much. I know we can get through anything together."

There was a long pause. Brad prepared himself for more questions. Instead, Roger reached out to shake his hand. "I don't have more questions, Brad. You pass! But once you take her, there is no giving her back!"

A pound of sweat dripped from Brad's body when he said, "Oh, don't worry about that."

The Fishing Trip

September 20, 1998

Brad knew exactly where and when he wanted to propose. This vision involved walking through the woods to his favorite fishing spot along Riley Creek. When he casually told Kim that he wanted her to go fishing with him that day, she looked forward to the time they could be together. Brad loved doing anything outdoors and although fishing wasn't at the top of her favorite things to do, she tried not to show it.

It was warm outside and her biggest concerns were sweating, her makeup running, and looking at gross worms she wouldn't think of touching. Then there were the issues of getting her black t-shirt and jeans dirty, not to mention mussing her hair. After tromping through the woods for what seemed like hours, she finally said, "How much farther, Brad? It's so hot out here."

"We're almost there. Just be patient."

A few minutes before she ran out of the little patience she could still muster, they reached the idyllic destination point. Unfortunately, Brad's hopes were diminished when he saw several others fishing in his favorite spot. Not to be deterred, he decided on a different spot.

Kim pretended to pay attention when he showed her how to cast the fishing line. She was more concerned that the worm would wiggle off the hook and land on her. When her casting efforts resulted in the hook being caught twice in the tree branches, Brad suggested they find a new location. "I know another good place to fish. It isn't far away." Kim just rolled her eyes. This was turning into a disaster; she couldn't fathom how he could be enjoying this.

Along the way, he spontaneously said, "Let's stop here." Kim didn't argue; she was just happy that they were nearly out of the woods. When he bent down on one knee and fumbled around trying to get something out of the tackle box, she finally said, "Brad, what are you doing? What do you need?"

Still on bended knee, he opened the jewelry box that had been safely stashed away; he looked up and said, "I need for you to say 'yes.' Will you marry me, Kim?"

She shouted with joy, "Yes, I'll marry you! Brad, you picked the ring I liked the best! I love you!" She touched his cheek and kissed him.

"Whew! That's a relief."

She looked at him in disbelief. "Why would you ever question my answer? You know I'm so in love with you."

"I was just so nervous. It's hard for me to say what I'm feeling. I was afraid I couldn't find the right words."

They kissed and his embrace lifted her off her feet. "You know you can't change your mind now, Kim. You're mine forever. There's no return policy. Your parents have given me permission to marry you and your dad said I can't give you back!"

"That's good to know! I'll remind you of that the next time I get the fishing hook caught in the branches and you get impatient with me."

He laughed and kissed her again. "Me? Impatient? Now we have the rest of our lives for me to teach you how to fish."

"Only on one condition," she teased. "I refuse to ever put the worm on the hook and that's final."

"Fair enough," he laughed.

"Brad, can we end this fishing trip now? I can't wait to tell our parents and show them my ring."

The wedding date was set one week later. They would become husband and wife on June 26, 1999. A few weeks before Brad proposed, Kim had said she'd like for them to both start keeping gratitude journals that shared their feelings for one another and the people they loved. He agreed to do it and bought the journals. She couldn't help but wonder what he would write as her elations poured onto the page.

I'm very grateful that Brad asked me to marry him today. I really can't imagine my life if he wasn't in it. I get chills in knowing that we'll get to spend the rest of our lives together. I love being loved by him.

I'm thankful for his sense of humor and that he treats me like a lady. Even though it might seem like a small thing that he opens the door for me, I appreciate this token of affection and respect. I'm thankful that he always accepts me for who I am. I'm grateful for his hugs and kisses and how he compliments me on what I'm wearing. I'm also grateful that he said he'll be doing most of the cooking when we're married!

I'm grateful for the time I get to spend with my mom, my dad, and my sisters. When I look at the things I wrote in my journal when I was fighting cancer, I took it for granted that they would be there to support me. I am so blessed.

I'm grateful to God for my life and for bringing Brad into it.

The Vows

June 26, 1999

Jackie was awake at dawn, knowing that so much work needed to be done before the wedding. With a cup of tea in hand, she went to the sunroom and looked at the 1.5 acres of backyard where Kim and Brad's wedding would be held. She smiled in knowing that Kim's dream to have an outdoor wedding at home was going to be realized at 7:30 that evening. She had been praying for days that it wouldn't rain, as she pictured 300 guests sitting under the open sky. Even though the weather forecast looked fairly promising, she was extremely relieved that arrangements had been made to have the ceremony at the church if need be.

Kim had carefully chosen the songs she wanted sung by her friends, Joy and Skyler, who she knew would do a wonderful job. One of her favorites was 'A Parent's Prayer' that she wanted her mother to sing. As much as Jackie wanted to honor her request, she knew she'd never be able to keep her composure. Instead, she recorded the song that would be played when she and Mary joined hands and lit a parents' candle, the symbol of their children's lives becoming one.

Jackie spent weeks pulling every visible weed from her flower beds and treasured the time spent with family and her many friends who helped turn the yard into the colorful paradise Kim envisioned; the vibrant flowers were in full bloom and proved to be a striking contrast against the backdrop of blue spruce trees that framed their land. The image that touched her most, however, was watching Roger spend endless hours designing and building a stage for the ceremony that rested in the corner of the yard facing the pine trees. It featured six white pillars they had rented and artificial grass that he tacked down to soften the overall look. Even though Brad and the whole family had been involved in helping him build this project, it was Roger's craftsmanship that turned the stage into a masterful piece of art.

When Kim had first shared that she wanted an outdoor wedding, Roger's eyes widened and he looked at Jackie for clarity. "Does this mean that the reception and dance will be in the shed?"

Jackie just smiled. "Yes, it does, honey. That means we need to start cleaning it up. Immediately!"

Although it seemed like an insurmountable task, they joined forces as a family and turned the shed into a spotless site that would accommodate the wedding party table, the food, the cake, the gift tables and several guest tables. They rented a large white canopy tent that was nestled against the shed and filled to capacity with more guest tables. Once the meal was finished, the shed would become the dance floor with plenty of room for guests to bring in chairs to watch and visit.

Jackie and her loyal team of supporters decorated the trees with strands of white lights; more were hung in the shed over the dance floor and on the wall decorations behind the head table. Fresh flowers were added to the white lace that draped majestically from one pillar to the other; colorful flower pots accented the yard that looked like a magical garden.

Shortly after the decorating was finally done, Jackie received a phone call from her good friend, Renee, who was in Ottawa, a town only 10 minutes away.

"Jackie, it's raining here right now. Don't worry about your decorations! I'll bring some tarps to cover them."

After Jackie prayed once again that it wouldn't rain, she did a final check on everything outside. Then she went into the house to get ready. She could hear laughter coming from Kim's bedroom in the basement. It was the bridal party that included Kim's sisters and friends, Sarah and Robin who were having so much fun getting ready. When Kim heard Jackie come in, she darted upstairs to show her the surprise that had arrived minutes earlier. Brad had sent a dozen light pink roses with a card that read: 'I can't wait until I see you tonight.'

She was so determined that Brad wouldn't get a glimpse of her until the ceremony that she had things timed perfectly with the photographer; he had set up a professional backdrop in the basement to capture some pictures before the wedding. Once he had taken several shots of Kim in her gorgeous gown and the attendants who looked absolutely beautiful in their dresses that were a rich eggplant hue, they scurried upstairs. While the photographer went outside to round up the guys, the bride couldn't resist sneaking a quick peek out the window to see how incredibly handsome her soon-to-be husband looked.

Kim wanted both of her parents to walk her down the aisle and minutes before the prelude began, Jackie and Roger reached for one another's hand and prayed. The photographer captured the serene moment. Included in the photo was a guest who was walking by at that precise moment. When he saw Jackie and Roger in prayer, he stopped and bowed his head.

In order for Brad not to see her until the last possible moment, Kim covertly slipped away from the back of the house and hid behind the front of the shed, while the bridesmaids made their way down the aisle. She couldn't have successfully pulled off this romantic caper without the help of her two accomplices, Jackie and Roger, who followed her lead.

Jackie couldn't resist peeking around the corner to watch the wedding party walk under the magnificent archway that was adorned with fragrant flowers and greenery. She did all that she could to delay the crescendo of tears that were reminders of all Kim had gone through. She and Roger were so thankful for Brad who they knew would be faithful and love their daughter 'till death do them part.'

As everyone stood in honor and turned to watch the elegant bride and her proud parents walk down the aisle, there wasn't a dry eye in the audience. Everyone had an emotional investment in this moment, whether it was through family ties, friendships or steadfast prayers. While this magnificent day was a celebration of marriage, it was also a celebration of Kim's precious life.

She was a stunning vision of beauty in her sleeveless white matte satin gown with a low back and chapel train; the A-line style featured a scoop neckline trimmed with pearls and sequins. Her hair was pulled up and accented by a pearl headpiece with a veil that glided gracefully down her back. She carried a large bouquet of white tulips with eggplant saffrons and cascading English ivy.

As her eyes welled with tears the closer she got to Brad, he was overcome by Kim's beauty and tilted his head ever so slightly in adoration. When Roger slowly let go of his daughter's hand, Brad reached for it. When they turned to face the pastor, he whispered, "You look so beautiful."

She smiled and whispered back, "Thank you for the surprise roses this morning."

Everyone's emotions were magnified when Jackie's friend, Carla, read a tribute to the couple that was based on verses from the book of Jeremiah.

"Just a few years ago, some might have questioned God's promise to Kim of a future but our God is a good and gracious God. He definitely has plans for Brad and Kim to prosper. Every good and perfect gift comes from our Heavenly Father. Brad and Kim are blessed with good and perfect gifts from above. They will never have to wonder if their marriage will work out because they have a promise from God that it will. Their union is of God, not of the world but a marriage covenant agreed upon by the two of them, whereas they are one flesh in the eyes of our Heavenly Father. Today we witness this marriage covenant that is a product of Christian parents who have prayed and believed for this day to come ever since their children were small. Let us all take a moment and pray in silence for their union and all marriage covenants represented here today. Let us give thanks for Brad and Kim, our mates, families, and friends, as we ask God to continue to bless, strengthen, and reveal His perfect plan for all of us."

As they exchanged vows, Kim's eyes glistened with tears. She was a young bride who had never been away from home and her family. While she felt a touch of sadness in walking away from this chapter of her life, she was excited about sharing her future with a man she couldn't have loved more. Once they were pronounced man and wife and Brad heard the words, "And now you may kiss the bride," he held Kim's face in his hands and kissed her tenderly.

By the end of the service, there hadn't been the slightest hint of rain. As the audience was invited to the reception, the bridal party was anxious for the photographer to take the pictures. The 90 degree heat was beginning to take a toll on the groomsmen who were sweating profusely in their tuxedos.

The night was filled with compliments and best wishes for the new couple. While they were dancing, Kim couldn't resist asking Brad if those were tears he was wiping from his eyes during their vows. He insisted it was sweat dripping from his brows. She just smiled and didn't believe a word of it.

As the dance and festivities were coming to a close, one of the guests made a special point to tell Kim how moved she had been by the entire evening. "Kim, I feel like I've seen heaven's beauty tonight."

"Thank you. I feel the same way. God provided us with a special day."

Shortly after midnight, everything had been cleaned up and put away. Even though Jackie and Roger were exhausted and looked forward to a good night's sleep, they sat on the swing under the trellis and gazed at the white lights that continued to sparkle. They were reflecting on the perfect night when the phone rang. It was Juleen who had just left minutes earlier.

"Jackie, you won't believe this. Dave and I are on our way home and all the roads are wet. It's like God held an umbrella over your yard until the wedding was over!"

Seconds later, Jackie and Roger felt sprinkles of rain.

A New Beginning

$\mathcal{B}$rad did a superb job in making all the arrangements to honeymoon in Gatlinburg, Tennessee, where they stayed in a cozy cabin perched high in the mountains. Their days were filled with nature walks, shopping, and eating out. One night, Brad cooked steaks and potatoes on the grill that were the best Kim had ever eaten. She mentioned this more than once as a gentle hint that he'd be doing most of the cooking in the future.

While they valued every moment spent together that week, they were eager to return home to the quaint log cabin they'd rented just outside of town. The house, which was barely visible from the road because of the long winding lane, sat on five acres of ground that included a pond. When the homeowner, Louise Niswander, needed to go to a nursing home, her children who lived out of state decided to rent the house and property.

Kim and Brad immediately grabbed the opportunity to live there. It was close to town yet secluded enough to have that country feel they wanted. Because the house had sat empty for several months, little had been done to maintain the property. When Brad asked Louise if she would like for him to clean up the outside area, she was delighted and whenever her daughter returned to visit, they would pull into the lane and marvel at the work that had been done.

Once they crossed the state line into Ohio, Kim's pulse quickened. "Brad, I'm so anxious to get home."

"Me too. I need to mow and do some more work around the pond."

Kim was struck by his words. She couldn't help but smile in knowing she had married a hard-working man with so much common sense - just like her dad.

"I love you, Brad."

"I love you, too."

Unexpected

Their first year of marriage went by quickly. Kim worked full-time at The Granary and Brad took a new job as a chemical operator in a nearby city. While living within their means, they began saving as much money as they could to one day build a home in the country. More importantly, they wanted to start a family.

In July of 2000, Kim shared this with Jackie and sought her advice. "Mom, Brad and I are hoping that I'm pregnant by this time next year. With my medical history, we aren't sure what type of fertility treatments I might need."

"Honey, before you start thinking about that, why don't you go off your birth control pill for a while and see how your body reacts? Let nature take its course until you have a period."

Nature took its course in a most unexpected way. When Kim didn't menstruate, she took a home pregnancy test that indicated she was pregnant. She and Brad were ecstatic and shocked; they never dreamed she'd be able to get pregnant so soon. At this same time, she had plans to travel out of state with her parents and sisters to visit family members. Because she wanted to be certain of the pregnancy before leaving, Jackie made quick arrangements at her doctors' office for an ultrasound; the test confirmed that she was four weeks along. Although it was too early to see a heartbeat, everything looked good.

When she and Brad went back to the doctor for her first consultation, she was six weeks pregnant and they were so anxious to see the baby's heartbeat. Tragically, there was no heartbeat. The doctor told them to come back in a week but the results were the same. Kim had a miscarriage.

September of 2000

My mind is flooded with painful emotions. I've gone from feeling overwhelming joy to overwhelming despair. I feel like a failure that my body couldn't carry a baby. I keep asking myself if I did something wrong or if God is mad at me. I feel embarrassed; we already started to tell people our amazing news and now we have to tell them our bad news. I feel jealous seeing other ladies having healthy pregnancies.

During that week between the two ultrasounds, I felt God speak to me when I was praying in church and telling Him how mad and sad I was. He made it very clear to me that I was not alone in losing the child I thought I was having and that He felt the same pain I was feeling. I'm going to try to change how I've been responding by remembering His message. In all honesty, this isn't easy to do.

Mom continues to reinforce how joyful and optimistic we need to remain that I was able to get pregnant. This is something the doctor said would probably never happen. It does make me wonder if we will have continual problems with multiple miscarriages. My doctor has suggested we wait three months before trying to get pregnant again.

Kim was pregnant four months later.

Tanner

*E*ven though Kim had a better feeling about this pregnancy, she was still fearful that she might miscarry again. These fears didn't subside until the first ultrasound. The moment she and Brad heard the baby's heartbeat, they sighed with relief. With each ultrasound that followed, they rejoiced in the miracle of seeing this new life develop fingers, toes, arms and legs.

Kim had morning sickness through the first half of the pregnancy and kept a sleeve of crackers and a drink beside the bed. She craved pizza, salsa and turtle sundaes that contributed to the 30 lbs. she gained. Even though she had a feeling all along that she was carrying a baby boy, they couldn't stand the suspense of not knowing for sure. An ultrasound midway through the pregnancy confirmed her maternal intuitions. They were going to have a boy. They already had his name picked out. He would be called 'Tanner' and his middle name would be 'Gladwin' after Brad's Grandpa Gladwin 'Pete' Smith. The day they learned they'd be having a son, Kim got out the new baby book and she and Brad each wrote messages to their son they couldn't wait to meet.

About Your Mom: *Well, Tanner, your mom was a very nice person until she met me. Then I became a nice guy! When I met your mother, she was quiet and sweet. This was a real change for me considering I was a rowdy senior and she was a shy sophomore. Everyone from day one thought we wouldn't last but I guess we fooled them. Your mother has a gigantic heart and is so kind. She keeps me in line and really changed my life for the good. Your mother cannot wait to see you for the first time and neither can I!*

About Your Dad: *Tanner, your dad was born on October 16, 1975. I imagine that he came into the world causing trouble and being a prankster. He loves to pick on people but actually has a heart of gold. He is a hard worker and has learned everything through trial and error. Your dad loves to hunt, fish, and play sports - anything to be outdoors. He always has to keep busy. He is an excellent cook! Thinking of your dad makes me smile. He has changed a lot from when we started dating to now. I'm so thankful God has given him to us. He will be an excellent father to you. I know his heart will melt the first time he sees you!*

Kim's due date was October 21st but she went into preterm labor on September 11, 2001. This was the heinous day that the country was attacked. She and her family were terrified when they heard a TV reporter say that one of the planes that had gone down departed from one of the airports in Boston. Roger was on a business trip and was scheduled to leave Boston that day. It wasn't until later in the afternoon that Jackie and the girls learned he was on a different flight and was safe. The worry had been overwhelming and this might have contributed to Kim's contractions.

She was admitted to the hospital later that day for observation.

While lying in the hospital bed that night, she watched the tragic scenes on TV in disbelief and sorrow. In seeing the country so vulnerable to such unconscionable acts of terrorism, she couldn't help but wonder about the future safety of the child in her womb.

Once the contractions stopped, Kim was released and put on bed rest for two weeks. The original plan was for her to be induced on Monday, October 8th after the doctor noticed on an earlier ultrasound that one of the baby's kidneys might not be functioning properly. This plan never evolved. Kim awakened at 12:30 a.m. on Sunday, October 7th, and discovered her water had broken.

Awaiting Tanner's birth: *As soon as my labor pains started, I woke up your dad and told him we needed to get to the hospital. He didn't believe me and quickly fell back asleep. So I called Mom and she said to start timing the contractions and when to go to the hospital. I woke your dad back up at 4 a.m. and made it clear that we needed to get to the hospital. I thought he would drive as quickly as possible but for some reason he decided to take his time which really perturbed me. Once I was admitted, he and the doctor started talking about the Ohio State Buckeyes and the Cleveland Browns! I just looked at them and thought, "Are you kidding me?"*

When it came time for me to have an epidural, your dad had to have the nurse escort him out of the room. He doesn't handle needles or blood well. Yes, he can skin a deer but he gets white as a ghost when he sees a needle.

After 10 hours of labor, I gave birth to you at 10:33 a.m. on October 7, 2001. You weighed 7 lbs. 10 oz. and were 20" long. You had striking dark hair. Once we were released from the hospital two days after you were born, this is what I wrote in your baby book about your big arrival: 'Oh, Tanner, I was so excited to have you! I couldn't wait to see what you were going to look like. You will always be the cutest baby boy ever. I love you so much. I look at you daily and thank God for you. You are so precious and have the most amazing blue eyes. You have been so lovable and easy-going.

Love you forever!
Mom

Motherhood

Special Memories

When I was pregnant with you, Tanner, your dad and I were in the process of building a house on 1.5 acres of land in the country. The fact that it was just down the road from my parents made the location even more ideal. As a soon-to-be-mother, I felt a welcomed sense of security in knowing my mother was nearby. A few weeks after you were born, we moved into our new home. I rejoice daily in being your mom.

You loved being rocked to sleep. I wrapped a soft Noah's ark blanket around you that was made by one of your Grandma Brinkman's friends. I nursed you for the first five weeks of your life and then started you on a bottle because I had to go back to work six weeks after you were born. We were so fortunate that Cindy Schumacher was your babysitter. She babysat for me and my sisters when we were young. Even though I knew you were in great hands, I cried all the way to work the first day I handed you to Cindy. At that time, I was working four days a week. Your dad was working a swing shift, so there were often a couple of days each week that he could be home with you. My mom watched you whenever she had a day off. You were surrounded by so much love and my sisters showered you with attention.

Your first words were "da-da" at six months old and "ma-ma" at eight months. You took your first steps when you were eleven months old. Your nicknames were 'Little Bean' or 'Beano' and others started calling you 'Tan-man.' We had a dog named Ruger and you thought it was funny when he licked you. You never sucked your thumb but always wanted a pacifier. Our goal was to have you off of it by the time you were eighteen months old. One day you and your dad were outside and you dropped it in the yard. Ruger snatched it up and ate it! The pacifier was no longer an issue.

When you were a toddler, it was apparent that you were always going to have a lot of energy. You loved swinging, taking walks in the stroller, climbing everything within reach and throwing any ball you could get your hands on. You and I spent hours sitting on the kitchen floor together where you'd say 'zoom zoom' as we raced your matchbox cars back and forth. You were your dad's loyal sidekick in whatever project he was working on outside and if you were within earshot of hearing Papa Brinkman start the tractor, you wanted to take a ride.

Your first birthday was memorable. Your Grandma Mary brought you a chocolate cake shaped like a teddy bear. As a precautionary measure, I took your clothes off and just had you in a diaper because I had a feeling that you would smear the icing all over your face. You were even more adventurous; the cake and icing found their way into your ears and up your nose. You weren't quite as messy with your second birthday cake that your Grandma

Oglesbee decorated to look like a football player. This time you enjoyed eating it with ice cream.

Your third birthday is only a month away. You haven't said what kind of cake you want yet. You're more interested in putting your hand on my tummy, especially when you can feel the baby moving. I keep telling you that you're going to be getting a baby sister very soon. You're going to be such a good big brother, Tanner.

Love you forever!
Mom

Avery

Monday, October 4, 2004

Dear Avery,

You were born today at 6:32 a.m. Your dad and I have never seen a more beautiful baby girl! You weigh 6 lbs. 11 oz. and are 19"long. You have dark brown hair that feels like silk and we marvel at how much you look like your brother who will be three years old in a few days. When Tanner saw you for the first time today, he reached out to touch your ears right away.

We knew ahead of time that you would be a girl. We were thrilled! Your dad and I had prayed to have a healthy boy and girl. We agreed immediately on naming you Avery Renee. We thought Avery would be a pretty girl's name and it sounded so nice with my middle name. In the months leading up to your birth, I wondered if it was possible to love another child as much as I love Tanner. The second I saw you, my heart overflowed with love. God seems to know how big a mother's heart should be to hold so much love for her children.

When we got to the hospital, your dad and I were surprised to see so many decorations in the room. Your Grandma Brinkman (who Tanner calls Nena) and my cousin, Amy, who works on the OB floor had personalized the walls with photos of your brother and pictures of bright flowers and pumpkins that he colored for you. Avery, I can't tell you how peaceful and comfortable it made me feel when I was only hours from giving birth to you.

At 2 a.m. I went to the bathroom and my water broke. This meant you were saying, "Mom, it's time!" Your dad and I called for the night nurse immediately. Much to our good fortune, the nurse was Lee Ann, a family friend. It didn't bother her a bit when she rushed into the room and my water leaked on her shoes. She was immediately in touch with the doctor who arrived about 30 minutes before you were born. This was a special night for her because she had accepted another job and you were the last baby she helped deliver.

I loved being pregnant with you, Avery, and your birth was so easy. The only unexpected moment was learning that the umbilical cord was wrapped around your neck. I lay there waiting to hear you cry. When you did, I praised God. I couldn't wait to hold you in my arms. It was so overwhelming to cradle your tiny body that God had knitted in my womb.

Your bedroom is already decorated. Weeks before you were born, your dad and my family all helped in painting your bedroom a light yellow color. I found a border for the walls with shades of yellow, white, blue, green and purple with these words written on it: Believe, Hope, Dream, Peace and Love. The words are accented with designs of daisies, butterflies, hearts and doves. It is perfect, Avery, because it is so pretty and serene. Your great-grandma

Oglesbee made bumper pads for your crib and a beautiful quilt in gingham check with squares of colors that match the purple, yellow and green colors in your bedroom.

I knew that I wanted a Bible verse to be painted above the shelf on the wall. Your Nena and I tossed around certain verses but nothing seemed to grab me until I read some verses from the book of Isaiah when the Lord declares that He has chosen each of us by name and that we are His.

I wrote the scripture on the wall in pencil and Nena painted the lettering in purple with a thin brush. I was especially picky with the way the capital 'A' was made, so I revised the letter until it looked perfect.

I look so forward to watching your personality evolve as you grow. We'll have so much girl time together like I did with my mom. I have a feeling that you'll probably be a Daddy's girl.

You are going to have the standard hearing test tomorrow that newborns are given. Then the day after that we get to go home! I can't wait to rock you and hold you close to my heart.

Love you forever!
Mom

Unprepared

$\mathcal{W}$hen the nurse walked into the room and told Kim and Brad that Avery failed the hearing test, they were so shocked that they didn't know what to say or ask. The thought that she could have hearing issues had never occurred to them. Their immediate concerns were somewhat quelled when the nurse said that they shouldn't worry about it. She explained that there might be fluid in her ears from birth that hadn't worked its way out yet and that the test would be repeated the next morning.

It was apparent by Kim and Brad's facial expressions that they didn't understand the specifics of the test and asked the nurse for more information. Avery had been given an Otoacoustic Emissions (OAEs) test that examined the function of the cochlea, her inner ear structure. They learned that when sound reaches the cochlea, hair cells in this organ produce a response called an emission that is like an echo. The presence of otoacoustic emissions usually indicates normal inner ear function. The absence of the emissions may indicate a problem in the middle or inner ear and/or a hearing loss.

Kim was awake early the next morning and started packing

her suitcase in anticipation of being discharged. On the way to the nurses' station to get Avery, she grew increasingly nervous when she asked, "Did Avery pass her hearing test?" She wasn't prepared to hear the nurse say, "She didn't pass it, Kim. The doctor will come to your room and talk to you and Brad before you're discharged."

Her eyes welled with helpless tears as she turned around and walked back to the room. She couldn't comprehend how this could be happening to her two-day-old daughter who was sleeping so peacefully. As Brad was on his way to the hospital, she felt herself losing control of her emotions and called her mother.

Jackie was taking a walk with her friend, Linda, when the cell phone rang. The instant she heard Kim crying, she sensed what was coming. "Mom, Avery failed the hearing test again. The doctor is going to talk to us. Brad is on his way. Can you please come? I'm scared."

"Honey, I'm on my way."

Jackie raced to the hospital. Although she hadn't voiced it, she had questioned the results of the first tests, even after talking to the doctors she worked for who also thought it was probably the extra fluid causing the hearing issues. As she pulled into the hospital parking lot, she took a deep breath and tried to ease the sickening feeling in the pit of her stomach.

Kim feared the doctor would deliver horrible news but that was not the case. She felt like she could breathe again when he said that 2 out of 10 newborns fail the screening due to fluid that remains in the ears after birth. As he signed the discharge papers, he told Kim they would repeat the screening in two weeks.

She tried to make herself believe that Avery would pass the next one, even though her maternal instincts told her differently. Whenever Avery wasn't sleeping, she sought every opportunity to make loud noises and watch her reactions. Kim had developed a cough after Avery's birth, so she repeatedly laid her on the living room floor and would sit on the nearby couch and cough as loudly as possible. She was encouraged that Avery was startled by the sounds every time.

When she put her seven-day-old daughter to bed, she held her cheek against Avery's and prayed: *"Lord, thank you for helping me in Avery's delivery that went so well. She is such a good baby and we are so connected. I know her hungry cry and her sleepy cry. Thank you for the gift of her life. Lord, please use me, however you see fit. I'm so grateful for the favors and blessings you have given us this past week."*

Kim did her best to try and be positive about the next screening but fear trumped hope when she was holding Avery in the waiting room. She had driven to the appointment by herself so that Brad could stay home with Tanner. Her decision to go alone was one she later regretted. She cried all the way home after the audiologist explained that Avery had failed the screening again and they would repeat the test in four weeks.

Avery slept soundly while Kim's worries melded into terrifying questions that invaded her mind. *What if Avery is playing in the driveway in a few years and the ball bounces onto the road? What if she runs to get the ball and can't hear the car coming? Will friends ever ask her to their houses for sleepovers when she can't even hear them? Will I ever hear her speak clearly or ever be able to hear her read a book to me? How am I going to tell our family and friends that our perfect little girl isn't perfect?*

Brad didn't have to ask how things had gone when Kim got home; he knew by her swollen eyes that it was more bad news. When she started crying uncontrollably, Jackie called the pastor to come pray with them that evening. He had previous commitments but his wife, LeAnn, offered to come. Even though Kim wanted to be able to say that she felt better immediately after the time spent in prayer, she couldn't. Even though she wanted to be able to trust that God would handle things for them in a positive way, she couldn't. As she looked at Avery each day, more terrifying thoughts played out in her mind. There was nothing she could do to escape them.

More Tests

In November of 2004, Kim and Brad took Avery back for the hearing test that she failed once again. At that point, they were referred to an ear, nose and throat specialist, who Kim knew well. That specialist was Dr. Robertson. Even though Kim respected him greatly and was so thankful for the crucial role he had played in saving her life, she dreaded the thought of sitting in his waiting room. Instead of being the frightened teenager, she was now the frightened mother.

As part of the consultation, Dr. Robertson asked a series of routine questions that included any risk factors Kim might have had during the pregnancy, if she carried Avery full term, if there had been any complications with her birth and if there was a history of hearing loss in the family. Kim grew more agitated with each question. She was so exhausted from worrisome, sleepless nights that she overreacted and found herself thinking, "How dare anyone ask questions that make me feel like I'm the one who has caused Avery's hearing complications!" When she shared her frustrations with Brad and Jackie after the appointment, they tried to assure her that the questions were necessary and she was taking things too personally.

Following Dr. Robertson's thorough examination of Avery's ears, he scheduled several other hearing tests that he wanted done in December. In the days leading up to the testing, Kim prayed for healing. She and Brad hoped for good test results that would enable them to move on with their lives.

At the same time that Avery was undergoing doctors' appointments and tests, other young mothers in Kim and Brad's church wanted to start a Bible study group. Kim was immediately interested and looked forward to the opportunity to form new friendships while learning more about the Bible. This group of young mothers sought Jackie's advice in how to structure their meetings because of her previous experience with Bible studies.

When Jackie dropped Kim off following one of the meetings, Kim finally verbalized the emotional pain she could no longer hide. Jackie immediately said, "Kim, you need to talk this over with God. You need to let Him know how you're feeling with all of this."

Kim sat in darkness on the edge of the bed that night and tearfully prayed: *"Lord, I don't know where to begin. I'm so mad that we have to deal with this. I question where you are in the midst of things. It's not fair that we have to go through this. I prayed for a healthy baby. Why didn't you give me that? What did we do to deserve this? Avery is a completely innocent baby. You gave my parents 16 years with me before they had to fully hand my life over to you when I had cancer. I've only been given a number of days before I'm supposed to hand my daughter and her life over to you."*

Avery was required to be asleep for two of the tests that Dr. Robertson ordered. Three electrodes were attached to her forehead and to each ear. They were then connected to a computer. As sounds were transmitted through the ear phones in her ears, the electrodes measured how her hearing nerves responded to the sounds. She was the perfect patient and slept for the exact length of time the tests required.

Kim and Brad sat in a dark, quiet room for several hours while Kim held Avery on her lap during the tests. They could hear the muffled sounds of Christmas music being played. When Kim excused herself to use the restroom, she stopped in the hallway immediately when she heard the lyrics of her favorite song - 'Awesome God.' She knew this was no coincidence.

Sadly, the test results indicated that Avery had a mild to moderate hearing loss that was conductive in nature. The audiologist explained that conductive hearing loss occurs when sound is not conducted efficiently through the outer ear canal to the eardrum and the tiny bones (ossicles) of the middle ear. She went on to explain that conductive hearing loss usually involves a reduction in sound level or the ability to hear faint sounds. With fluid in the ears being one of the major causes of conductive hearing loss, Dr. Robertson advised that Avery undergo a surgery to have pressure-equalization tubes put in her ears when she was six months old.

Different emotions emerged in trying to process all the information. Kim began to feel jealous of other babies who were Avery's age. She couldn't understand why these parents were spared the devastating reality that she and Brad were facing. With each day that passed, her faith weakened. Her mind was filled with an angst she shared with no one. She wished she knew someone who was walking in her shoes and could empathize with her frustration, pain and despair. As she successfully hid the brittle emotions that consumed her, she continued to be active in her Bible study group. She attended church every Sunday and outwardly praised a God she thought had abandoned her. As she sang the songs of His grace, mercy, righteousness and power, she felt little comfort in the words that she found hard to believe.

Reminders

*T*he harder Kim tried to disguise her agony, the more apparent it became to her family. They knew her heart had closed the door on God, so they began reminding her of His presence with words of encouragement. Jackie often wrote Bible verses and prayers on index cards for Kim to carry with her and lay throughout the house. Her sister, Joy, wrote her a letter a few weeks after Avery's birth.

Dear Kim,

We may not understand why this is happening but God is at work here and will take care of all your needs. Please don't blame yourself...you had a great pregnancy and no one believes that you alone had any part in this. Avery is a beautiful little baby and I love her so very much. You have an awesome husband who loves you, Tanner, and Avery with all his heart. Keep in mind how lucky you are.

According to the doctors all those years ago, you might not have been able to have kids. Look how God has fixed that! This whole situation might be a road block in the way of her future but we will all be on that road with you and Avery. God has chosen a loving family to deal with this. We were strong enough to get you through Hodgkin's disease and we can get you through this. I know that Avery might not be able to hear your voice but she can see and feel your loving arms when you hold her.

Love,
Joy

Not long after receiving Joy's letter, Kim's cousin, Amy, sent her an email:

Avery is a beautiful little girl who has been entrusted to two wonderful parents and a brother who God knows is well capable of managing this obstacle, Kim. Whether it is temporary, permanent, partial or full hearing loss, she will be loved and cared for by a wonderful family and extended family.

I value your relationship with the Lord and know that He must think an awful lot of your witness to put so much of a burden on you. Without trials there is no growth and you have been presented with many trials in your life. How you have handled them has been a witness to your family, friends, and those you may not even know. We are grateful for your life and the lives of your children. Please know that we love you guys and will pray for you often.

Love,
Amy

Kim could feel the presence of the Holy Spirit speaking to her through the people around her. She sensed this even more each time she read the verse that was written on the wall above Avery's crib. It was a peaceful reminder that she was a gift and that Kim had been chosen to be her mother, her loving caregiver on this earth.

Inconclusive

By the spring of 2005, Avery's pleasant personality began to emerge. Her sparkling blue eyes accented the noticeable dimples in her chubby cheeks. In May, she underwent surgery to have tubes placed in her ears. Even though Kim knew this was a necessity, she sobbed when Avery was wheeled to the operating room. They were relieved beyond measure when told that she did well and that the doctor had been able to withdraw some fluid.

The next doctor's appointment in June involved repeating some tests, as well as giving Avery a new test called the Visual Reinforcement Audiometry (VRA). This behavioral audiometric test took place in a sound-treated room. Kim was instructed to hold Avery on her lap in a chair that was placed between two calibrated loudspeakers. The VRA used lighted and/or animated toys that flashed on simultaneously with the auditory signal. The toy was activated immediately after the child turned toward the auditory signal. It took so much self-restraint for Kim not to help Avery by pointing in the direction of the sound.

Kim's frustrations mounted when the culmination of tests came back inconclusive; she was told to bring Avery back in

August for more testing. The appointment went much better than anticipated. She and Brad actually left the office that day feeling very hopeful, especially when the audiologist's report stated that Avery's hearing was 'essentially normal.' The repeated VRA test showed that she was within normal hearing limits. Even though she failed the OAE test again, they were told this might have been due to the tubes in her ears.

For the first time since learning that Avery might have hearing problems, Kim felt a sense of freedom. They could now have a respite from doctors' appointments and didn't need to schedule another appointment for a year, unless they saw changes in her hearing or the lack of development in her speech.

This sense of relief didn't last long when Avery's primary care doctor thought she might have a possible heart murmur. Kim's emotions unraveled again and it affected her health both mentally and physically. She couldn't sleep through the night until tests determined that there was no heart murmur.

Once this worry was behind them, another emerged. There was concern over Avery's lack of growth. They met with a pediatric endocrinologist who suggested that genetic testing be done, in addition to testing that would indicate her growth hormone functions.

The first day of tests took three hours and involved drawing several samples of her blood. In following the specialist's orders, they returned two weeks later where she was once again subjected to three hours of testing that required many more blood draws. It was excruciating to watch her go through this even though she was remarkably brave during the procedures.

The results were inconclusive again. While one test indicated she produced sufficient growth hormones, the other test showed she didn't. When the endocrinologist suggested that she undergo one more test that would be similar to the others, Kim and Brad decided it was time to step back. From the beginning, they weren't comfortable with giving her growth hormone medication. They rationalized that there was no reason to expect her to be very tall because they weren't. Instead, they decided to buy a growth chart and monitor her progress at home.

While all of this was going on, it was very apparent that Avery's speech was significantly delayed. When it became extremely difficult to understand what she was saying, Kim's prayers changed direction. Instead of asking God to heal Avery's hearing loss, she prayed that He would help her speak and hear more clearly in order to communicate.

Empathy

As Kim was fighting her own emotional battle, her Aunt Juleen told her about two parents she knew whose baby was also born with a hearing impairment. Kim could empathize with everything they were dealing with and reached out to help them in a personal letter.

Hello Joe and Amanda,

My name is Kim Smith. I am Juleen Walters' niece. She recently told me what you've been going through with your baby, Beau. Because we went through similar circumstances a little over a year ago, she thought maybe you could benefit from hearing how we coped and what we went through.

When our second child, Avery, was born on Oct. 4, 2004, she also did not pass the hearing screenings (the OAEs) at the hospital. I was immediately shocked! I wasn't expecting my baby girl to have anything wrong with her. The doctor didn't seem too concerned and told us to bring her back in two weeks to be tested again. When she failed the follow-up test, I was absolutely shocked! I spent so much time crying that by the end of the day, I felt like I had been run over by a truck.

Avery was retested in four weeks and failed again. She was not even responding to 70 decibels which indicated severe hearing loss. During this time, I could feel the oppression that Satan was putting on me. I envisioned Avery starting to cross a street and not being able to hear a car coming; I envisioned her not hearing me when I shouted for her to stop. I pictured kids at school making fun of her for having to wear hearing aids. (See, I really was crazy!) I was so angry at God because I knew it was possible that I may never hear her say 'Mommy' or 'I love you.'

We were referred to an ENT who ordered two tests that were different from the OAEs. One test indicated she had mild to moderate hearing loss. When she was given a test where the sound bypassed the middle ear and went directly to the inner ear, she heard all the pitches perfectly. So we knew that we were dealing with a middle ear problem. At this point, we were told that there might be fluid in the ears. In May, she had surgery where tubes were inserted. We were very glad to hear the doctor come out of surgery and say he had drained some fluid.

We went back for her post-op visit in June. Out of a series of four tests, she passed two and failed two. The audiologist couldn't really say that she needed hearing aids but also couldn't really say that she didn't need them. At that point, the audiologist thought that Avery is among the 2% of the population that doesn't have all the tiny hair cells around the cochlea that the OAEs tests for. On the final report, the diagnosis was that Avery had 'essentially normal hearing.' This was such a joyous day after 10 months of going through so much.

I don't know how your situation is going to play out but I do know that we serve a great and mighty God. During the times when I needed comfort the most, He provided it. Whether it was through a song or a TV show, He was there. He is there for you, too. I can about guarantee that anything you are feeling right now, I've felt too.

I pray that you both will find that comfort when you need it the most. Please feel free to email me back or call to chat. I've included my phone number and a picture of our family so that you can put faces to the names. My husband's name is Brad and our son's name is Tanner.

Sincerely,
Kim

The Darkness of Denial

*W*hen Avery was eighteen months old, she was admitted to the hospital twice within a two-week period for dehydration and a urinary tract infection. When her body weight dropped to 18 lbs. and she lay lifeless in the hospital bed, Kim panicked. She couldn't juggle all these worries at once and found herself denying even further the issue that needed her attention the most - Avery's hearing impairment.

Shortly after Avery's birth, Kim and Brad were told that babies with hearing loss could be fitted with hearing aids as early as six months old. When the people from the Regional Infant Hearing Program got in touch with them, Kim was not interested because she continued to believe that Avery could one day function at the same level as other toddlers her age. This program (RIHPs) is funded through the Ohio Department of Health and provides services to families with babies and toddlers identified with a permanent hearing loss. There is no charge for these services that include: weekly home visits that teach families how to communicate with their infants and toddlers through play and daily routines, presenting information about available communication options; making referrals to service providers such as speech-language pathologists, audiologists and physicians, working with local Help Me Grow programs that provide health and developmental support so children can start school healthy and ready to learn; and information on available resources for children with hearing loss after the age of three years. While Kim acknowledged how beneficial it would be to families who needed the support, she didn't feel her family did.

Jackie and Roger were concerned early on that there was a serious problem with Avery's hearing. They were also concerned about her growth pattern. Jackie kept asking why Avery wasn't being fitted with hearing aids and said that all of them as a family would take sign language classes if that would help. Kim never acknowledged the questions and chose not to share her feelings, knowing that her mother's response would be very candid. This would mean having to hear the truth and that was something Kim was trying to escape.

Jackie cried many tears for Kim and Avery. She hated what they were going through. At one point, she asked Kim if she thought she was in depression. Jackie reminded her that there were medications that could help. She also stressed that being depressed was not a sign of weakness - that she was a young mother and wife who was yet again facing an incredible amount of stress in many areas of her life. When she and Roger offered to pay for any tests or therapies that weren't covered by their insurance, Kim wasn't receptive because she feared more testing could indicate something else might be wrong with Avery.

At the core of Kim's fragile emotions and broken heart was the guilt she had harbored ever since Avery failed her first hearing test. As the weeks and months of tests progressed, she became more and more defensive when the medical professionals asked questions regarding her own health and her pregnancy. Jackie and Brad told her repeatedly that the specialists were just doing their jobs and that no one ever insinuated it was her fault. She knew they meant well but the guilt continued to fester.

Therapy

By now, Avery was two years old and it was nearly impossible for Kim and Brad to understand anything she was trying to communicate. More times than not, Tanner was able to interpret what she was trying to say. The family doctor suggested they meet with a speech therapist. Following the evaluation, the therapist encouraged Kim to enroll her in the county's Help Me Grow program that was available for children from birth to age three who needed assistance with skills that included talking, walking, moving, hearing or behavior.

Avery was able to benefit from speech therapy for a year. Kim benefitted from the program as well. She felt empathy in being around other families whose children struggled with speech and hearing issues; she quickly realized that many families had children facing various health struggles that were far worse than Avery's.

Kim's mind-set began to change and she was anxious to share this with Brad. "I'm so thankful she's in this program. Even though she's only eligible for one year, I know it's really going to help her. The staff is so professional and friendly. They've already given me some handouts of things we should do at home to help her. I have such a good feeling about this, Brad."

When that year of speech therapy ended, the speech therapist and professionals at the Putnam County Educational Service Center suggested that Kim enroll her in preschool that was offered through the Columbus Grove school system. This way she could continue to receive speech therapy and would also have the opportunity to develop social skills by interacting with other children.

In order for Avery to be part of this early intervention, Kim met with the preschool teacher and professionals from the Educational Service Center to develop an Individualized Education Program (IEP) for Avery. The purpose of the IEP is to help children with delayed skills or disabilities succeed in school. Each IEP is crafted to specifically address the child's needs. Avery's IEP was especially designed to aid her in developing communication skills.

When the IEP team members asked how Avery communicated at home, Kim shared that Avery got her attention by saying 'Mom' and making eye contact with her. When she was unable to understand what Avery was trying to say, she would either point at an object or lead Kim to it. When asked to describe her concerns with Avery's daily skills, Kim was candid. "I think it has to be extremely difficult for others to understand what she's saying and what she wants. She certainly tries to mimic what we say and some words have gotten better. I have to continually ask her to slow down and repeat things. It's frustrating for all of us, especially Avery."

Reality

During a return check-up with the audiologist in 2007, Avery's tests indicated a hearing loss again. In order to prevent fluid from accumulating, it was recommended that she have another set of tubes put in her ears and also have her adenoids removed. In April of 2008, she underwent surgery for these procedures.

Two months later, Brad took Avery to her post-op appointment on his scheduled day off work. After looking at her test results, the audiologist advised that she be fitted for hearing aids. Brad called Kim at work to let her know how well things had gone; he explained that ear molds had been made for Avery's hearing aids that would be dark brown to blend with her hair. Kim was shocked! She couldn't believe how accepting Brad was with all of this.

Instead of questioning his judgment over the phone and growing more upset, Kim called the physician's assistant on her way home. She pulled off on a side road so that she wasn't distracted and could listen carefully to the words that she didn't want to hear. "Mrs. Smith, there is no way that Avery is going to be able to speak clearly until her hearing issues are corrected with hearing aids."

By the time Kim arrived home in tears, she was distraught

and took these feelings out on Brad who was fixing supper.

"Brad, what are you going to tell people when they see Avery with hearing aids? What is this going to mean for swimming parties and sleepovers? Kids are so cruel and they are going to make fun of her at school. How are we going to pay for all this when our insurance doesn't cover them? Have you thought about any of this?"

He looked at her and firmly said, "Kim, who cares what others think about her hearing aids? If they're going to help her, then that's what we need to do. I just want her to hear better and start to talk better so we can understand her. You need to get over this!"

Kim broke down in his arms and stayed there until she shed the many guilty tears she had been hiding far too long. Later that evening, she called her mother with the test results and the recommendation for hearing aids. Jackie immediately heard the panic in her voice. "Honey, I'm coming over."

Jackie knew it was imperative to support everything Brad said. His sentiments mirrored what she and Roger had been thinking for a very long time. The moment she arrived, Kim started crying. Jackie held her and said with conviction, "Honey, if Avery senses that you're embarrassed with her having hearing aids, she's also going to be embarrassed wearing them. She's going to need to see you be okay with her having them and being okay to talk about them around other people. You're going to have to embrace this and make it a good thing for her."

Although Avery was far too young to realize it, her life was going to change significantly when her mother stepped out of denial and prayed: *"Lord, I need your help. Avery needs your help. Tell me what to do. I'm listening. I continue to pray that you will miraculously heal her but I've finally accepted that she needs hearing aids. At this very moment, I pray for cleansing that will wash away all my guilt. You know far better than I what lies ahead in Avery's future. Whatever it is, she will be surrounded by love and support. Thank you for Avery, dear Lord. Thank you for my hero. Amen."*

Awakening

June of 2008

Kim was filled with anxiety when it was time to pick up the hearing aids. As the audiologist thoroughly explained all the parts and their functions, she wondered how she'd ever be able to remember everything. She felt overwhelmed with all the necessary information about keeping them dry, changing the batteries, and taking them out during her nap times and at bedtime.

Avery was as calm as her mother was nervous when the audiologist put them in her ears; she made no attempt to pull them out. Then it was Kim's turn to learn the procedure. Her hands shook in fear that she'd break them or cause Avery discomfort. Instead, Avery sat very still and Kim put them in perfectly on the first try.

With the hearing aids in place, it was obvious that the audiologist was excited to test Avery's hearing in the soundproof booth. Kim prayed the entire time. The results were conclusive. For the first time in Avery's young life, she passed the test; she was hearing within the normal limits. It wouldn't be long until she could point to the sky when she heard an airplane flying overhead.

Kim couldn't wait to get home and share the wonderful news

with Brad and their families. Everyone was relieved and hopeful that she'd quickly learn how to communicate more clearly. It immediately became apparent that this wasn't going to happen.

The frustrations mounted for Avery and everyone in the family when they tried to help by correcting her speech or asking her to repeat things. She refused to try quite often and would bury her face in her hands. Many times Kim felt defeated and frequently shared this with Jackie. "Mom, there isn't anything Brad and I can do when she shuts down. It feels like we aren't getting anywhere. I appreciate her preschool teachers so much. I just don't have the patience they do. I need to keep reminding myself that she hasn't been able to hear normally for three years, so I shouldn't expect her to talk clearly so soon."

"You and Brad are doing everything you can. She's saying the words that she was hearing before she got her hearing aids. In her mind, she's saying them correctly."

"I know," Kim sighed. "Many of the words she does use are hard to understand because she drops the beginning and ending sounds or substitutes sounds that make sense to her. Her teacher said she has trouble sitting still to listen to a story. It breaks my heart that she can't follow what's being said. That's why she's never been interested in watching TV. The conversation moves too quickly and she can't understand it."

By the end of the first year of preschool, Avery was able to understand simple conversation better but there was little gain in her ability to articulate her thoughts and needs. Kim and Brad were very receptive when her teachers and the IEP team recommended that she return for a second year.

Evaluations

$\mathcal{I}$n the fall of 2008, Avery started preschool with her hearing aids; they were the keys that unlocked a treasure chest of new sounds she reveled in discovering. She was now four years old and was able to keep up with her classmates in the areas of cognitive learning skills and motor skills. She was able to perform age-appropriate activities and follow the teachers' directions, as well as draw distinguishable objects and physically kick and throw a ball. Her outgoing personality blossomed even more when she interacted well with the other children.

Even though she was learning many new words and trying to verbalize them, it was still very difficult to understand what she was saying. When Kim met with the IEP team at the end of the second year of preschool, the discussion focused on ways to help improve her communication skills. It was a necessity for her to practice imitating speech sounds and the use of consonant and vowel combinations to produce sounds and words. When the team recommended that she return for a third year of preschool where she would continue to receive speech therapy and be involved in language-rich activities, Kim concurred immediately. She and Brad had seen so much improvement in her speech after two years of preschool that they welcomed the opportunity for more growth, knowing that it wouldn't be long until she started kindergarten.

Because Avery was on an IEP, she was required to undergo a Multi-Factored Evaluation (MFE) when she was five years old that thoroughly assessed her abilities and needs. Kim and Brad took her to the Ohio School for the Deaf in Columbus, Ohio, where she was evaluated in several areas that included psychological, academic, vision, fine and gross motor skills, functional behavior, social-emotional status, communicative status and auditory abilities. The comprehensive auditory test assessed how well she could hear in noisy environments and how she was processing the sounds she heard.

This evaluation was invaluable for the teachers, the IEP team and school administrators in knowing how to specifically address Avery's needs in the classroom setting. When Kim and Brad received the results, they were anxious to share the news with their parents.

Kim called Jackie immediately with the good news. "Mom, I don't know where to start. Brad and I are so relieved and so proud of Avery. There were a lot of tests and she cooperated on every single one. The results confirmed what we already knew. She has mild to moderate conductive hearing loss in both ears and should wear her hearing aids all day and only take them out at bedtime or if she goes swimming. The thing we're most excited about is that they've recommended the school buy a personal FM system that will bring the teacher's voice directly to her hearing aids through a wireless FM signal. When she starts kindergarten next year, her teacher will speak into a small lapel microphone that is linked to a transmitter that sends the signal to tiny receivers on Avery's hearing aids. She'll be able to hear the teacher, even if there is a lot of background noise in the room. This feels like a miracle. I've been so nervous about her going to kindergarten. Now I'm filled with relief. We know it's going to be hard for her to keep up with all the work but her chances of succeeding are so much greater now."

The Picnic

*A*very was excited for the last day of preschool because her class was having a picnic in the park and the children's families were invited to attend. The minute she saw her mom walk into the room, she hugged her around the waist.

"Mom, this is going to be really fun. After we all eat lunch, our teachers have a surprise for us."

While Kim enjoyed every moment of the afternoon, it was especially endearing to see how well Avery interacted with her classmates. She was no longer the affectionate little girl who couldn't communicate because she couldn't hear what was happening around her. She was now the affectionate little girl who looked forward to wearing her hearing aids - the little girl who could now speak with much more clarity.

As the afternoon was coming to an end, the teachers singled out each student and shared what they appreciated most about each one. Then they called each student forward and surprised them with personal scrapbooks of their school work.

After Kim thanked the staff for their incredible efforts in helping Avery the past three years, they responded with sincerity.

"We'll miss her, Kim. We enjoyed Avery so much." Then they made a point of saying, "Avery, if you see us next year, be sure and say hello."

As they walked to the car, Kim said, "Are you sad that it's your last day with your teachers, sweetie? They were so nice."

"They were really nice, Mom, but I'm not sad preschool is over. I'm glad it's summer so I can play T-ball and go swimming."

"Dad and I appreciate all the things they taught you."

"Yeah, I learned a bunch of new stuff and I can talk a lot better now, huh?"

"Oh, Avery, you can talk so much better! Dad and I are so proud of you and how hard you've worked."

"I know! I'm proud of me too!"

Kindergarten

A week before school started, Kim and Brad arranged to meet with the elementary principal, Avery's teacher, the intervention specialist and the audiologist who the county had contracted to oversee Avery's FM system. It was essential for everyone to be familiar with how it operated prior to the first day of school.

The audiologist demonstrated how a small silver receiver needed to be inserted at the bottom of each hearing aid every morning. Then it was crucial that the system be tested with the microphone that her teacher, Mrs. Selhorst, would wear. The last step involved putting the hearing aids in Avery's ears. As Mrs. Selhorst and Mrs. Roeder, the intervention specialist, practiced the procedure, Avery sat very still which helped a great deal. The team determined that it would work well for Mrs. Roeder to come to the classroom each morning and insert the receivers, as well as remove them at the end of the day when she worked one-on-one with Avery to reinforce various learning skills. In addition to the extra academic help she'd receive, a speech therapist from the county would work with her at different intervals throughout the week.

Because Avery would be receiving all this positive

reinforcement, Kim and Brad were looking forward to the start of the school year. They were also keenly aware that her learning skills lagged behind most of her classmates.

"Brad, I have a feeling that Avery is much farther behind than we realize. Many kids her age can count to 20, know how to write their names and can tell the difference between different shapes. Right now she can count to five and has a hard time printing her first name because she can't form all the letters correctly. She knows the names of most shapes but we need to help her learn the difference between a rectangle and a diamond - and to recognize the colors 'green' and 'white.' So much is expected of kindergarteners now. I pray she can handle everything."

"That's why she's on an IEP, Kim. She needs extra help. That's just the way it is."

"I know but it's still hard not to worry. She was too young in preschool to know if kids were making fun of the way she talked. Her feelings are going to be hurt now and I won't be there to protect her. I knew this day would come and I'm not ready for it."

"She'll be fine."

Kim anticipated that Avery would be excited to start school, especially after meeting her principal, Mr. Kincaid, and her teachers. That proved to be an understatement. Avery was exuberant.

"Mom, I can't wait for tomorrow! School is going to be so much fun. I'm lucky my two good friends are in my class. We can eat lunch together and play at recess. I have the same teacher that Tanner had. He said Mrs. Selhorst is real nice. I like Mrs. Roeder a lot too. She'll give me extra help when I don't understand things."

"Avery, if you don't stop talking and let me tuck you in, you'll be too tired to get up for school tomorrow."

"I'm too excited to sleep. I can't wait to see Hannah and my other friends. It's going to be so much fun!"

That first day of school was filled with the excitement Avery had anticipated and she talked nonstop about it at the supper table. "Mrs. Selhorst is so nice and it's fun eating lunch in the cafeteria with my friends. Recess is a blast. Some kids asked Mrs. Roeder what she was doing with my hearing aids this morning and she told them it was something that helps me hear better. I even get to pick one or two kids in my class to go with me to Mrs. Roeder's room at the end of the day. I need to learn how to tie my shoes. Lots of kids in my room already know how. I bet Mrs. Selhorst will be really proud of me when I can do it."

Three weeks into the school year, Kim got halfway to work when she realized that she'd forgotten to put in Avery's hearing aids. She turned around immediately, knowing Avery would panic as soon as she realized she didn't have them. She called the school secretary and explained what had happened and asked if she could get a message to Avery and her teacher that she was bringing them right away.

As soon as Avery saw Kim standing in the classroom doorway, she ran to her and started crying. "Mom, when I was on the bus I knew we forgot my hearing aids. I was scared."

"Honey, I'm so sorry. This won't ever happen again. We're going to tape a note to the door that says 'hearings aids.' Whenever your dad and I go out the door, it will be a reminder for us to make sure you have them in. You're okay now and the rest of the day will be fine. Let me wipe away your tears so you can go back to class."

"Mom, we need to write the note in really big letters so we never forget again."

"We will, sweetie. I promise."

As traumatic as this day had been for Avery, a thrilling one awaited her a few weeks later when she showed Mrs. Selhorst that she could tie her shoes. This was an achievement to be celebrated. When Avery returned to school the next day, Mrs. Selhorst surprised her with a pair of bright, multi-colored shoestrings. The kindergartener wore them proudly and didn't hesitate to share her accomplishment every chance she got.

Teamwork

$\mathcal{K}$im worked diligently with Avery every night to reinforce writing the letters of the alphabet correctly and pronouncing new sounds she wasn't able to articulate clearly. While many nights ended in frustration, she remained positive because of the open lines of communication she had established with Mrs. Selhorst and Mrs. Roeder through emails.

Monday, November 08, 2010 3:15 PM

Kim, I just finished playing a game with Avery, so I wanted to send you a quick message while I was thinking about this. They started the letter 'S' in class today, so we were playing with beginning sounds that start with the letter 'S.' For a word like 'spoon,' Avery says 'poon' so she says it starts with a 'p.'

By the time we were finished playing the game, she was saying it correctly, so I thought I would tell you so that you can continue trying to work on this when she is helping you set the table and so on. Obviously, when she leaves out the first sound in saying the word, it affects what she thinks the word starts with. If she can continue correcting herself at home that would help. This is just one word that really stood out to me today and that's why I wanted to email you. I can see so much improvement each day! Thanks for your help!

Mrs. Roeder

Monday, November 08, 2010 10:00 PM

Thank you for your email, Mrs. Roeder. It's funny that you picked up on this today. I noticed that all of her 'S' written papers came home today where she's making the 'S' backwards. So we worked on writing it correctly tonight. When she said the word for 'sock' she said 'tock' so I can identify with what you mean. It actually crossed my mind that maybe this happens more frequently with other papers she did last week that came home wrong.

I also reminded her that when she's doing some of the letter and number papers to look at the walls in the classroom for help in remembering how to write them correctly. And of course, I told her to take her time! I notice that when she's counting and marking the picture off with a slash, she often just keeps counting, regardless of what her pencil is doing with the slashes instead of making the counting and the slashing coincide. So obviously she gets it wrong. If you don't mind, could you share this information with Mrs. Selhorst? I look forward to talking with her at the parent/teacher conferences. These were two areas I was going to bring up.

We can definitely see improvements each week too. The letter of the week has been so helpful. You don't know how much we appreciate all that you and Mrs. Selhorst do for her each day. The journey of her little six-year-old life has not been an easy one but you both make sending her to school much easier each morning, knowing that you're there offering the best to her. Thanks so much!

Kim

Sunday, March 27, 2011 9:12 PM

Mrs. Selhorst, we had the chance this weekend to work on some of the school papers that Avery has brought home for extra practice. There were a couple of words that I noticed she had wrong and realized that if she says the words like she's always said them... which is not always the correct way, she uses them with different letters. For example, with the word 'game' she says 'dame' and therefore thought it started with a 'd.' The other ones were 'shew' for 'shell' and 'sot' for 'sock.' Thankfully, once I said the word correctly for her, she realized what letter was really correct. Thank you for sending those home. Not only is this all good for her to learn the beginning and ending sounds but it also helps along with her speech and saying things correctly.

I hope you have a good day and thanks again for all that you do each day!

Kim

Wednesday, March 30, 2011 11:46 AM

Hi Kim.

I've noticed the same thing. I agree that working on these skills (seeing the letter in print and also saying them aloud) does indeed help her speech. This is a big reason why I believe that the extra help she receives is so important...not because she doesn't "get" the skill but to help point out the discrepancies to her and why things are counted incorrectly.

I've also spoken with our county school psychologist about plans for Avery next year and what type of support she will be receiving. The plan is to continue with things similarly to this year (provide one-on-one/small group help but not to pull Avery away from the group during key instruction times). We also discussed having her first grade teacher established so that she can be a part of Avery's upcoming IEP meeting. This way we can all be on the same page at the beginning of next year and share ideas.

As an additional note, I've thought of a new type of activity for Avery to help her become more active when I ask comprehension questions to orally read stories. Would it be possible for me on Tuesdays to send home the story we will be reading on Thursdays with a list of questions I plan to ask the kids? This way the two of you could read it and take the time to discuss the questions. She could then answer in the large group settings with confidence. Also, when I read the story it will be the second time she hears it so the sequence and things of that nature would be reiterated. If you have any questions, please let me know.

Thank you for all your extra help at home!

Mrs. Selhorst

Throughout the year, Kim often wondered how Avery compared academically to her classmates. She feared that all the other children were progressing significantly more. While she had come so far in accepting Avery's impairment, shreds of denial resurfaced periodically. One night she confessed this in prayer. *"Lord, I have moments where I still want to compare Avery's learning abilities to others her age. I know this is unfair to her. I have to get completely past this. You know why I've felt conflicted at times. It really isn't about Avery's personal struggles. It's about my own personal struggles. All my life I've felt the need to compare myself to others because I lack self-confidence. I need to be comfortable in being your daughter - the person you designed me to be and not the person I've tried to be in order to feel accepted. I realize how crucial it is for Avery to feel good about herself. It's my responsibility to make sure this happens as I come to you in prayer each day and give thanks for her precious life. In Jesus' name I pray. Amen."*

During the second half of the school year, some of Avery's homework included reading short books at night. While they might have only been a few pages in length, her ability to do this reflected the remarkable progress she'd made. Even though Kim needed to help her with many of the words, Avery was able to read aloud on her own and delighted in hearing her mom say, "I love listening to you read."

When the school year ended, Kim enrolled her in the county's six-week summer speech camp that she had participated in the previous summers. In addition to attending camp two days a week, Avery also received a great deal of therapy at an area hospital every other week during the school year. Kim made sure that she experienced every language-enriched opportunity that was available.

First Grade

Dear Avery,

My mother always wrote me personal letters when she and Dad were proud of my achievements and during difficult times in my life when I needed words of encouragement. Those letters are keepsakes and that's what I want this letter to be for you.

You and Tanner are growing up much too quickly. Dad and I feel like the luckiest parents in the world and I thank God daily for the blessings of your lives. I don't know how it's possible that you've just completed first grade. You would say that your favorite part of the year was in the fall when you were a cheerleader for Tanner's midget football team that your dad helped coach. I loved sitting in the stands on Sunday afternoons and listening to you belt out your enthusiastic cheers. I smiled so often when you mixed in movements that were uniquely your own.

Do you remember when I gave you a great big hug when I saw you dressed in your red and white cheerleading outfit for the first time? You looked darling and your excitement was contagious. I waited to hear what you wanted me to do with your hair. This needed to be your decision. You never wanted it pulled back during school because you didn't want the other kids to see your hearing aids. You were afraid of being teased. You'll never know the tears of admiration and joy that overwhelmed me when you said, "Mom, I want you to pull my hair back in a ponytail like the other cheerleaders. Put the clip in my hair so I match everybody else."

Your experiences in first grade were as wonderful as those you had in kindergarten. You loved your teacher, Mrs. Haselman, and your intervention specialist, Mrs. Hazelton. They kept me informed continually of the progress you were making and the areas in reading and math where you were falling behind. They always offered suggestions how I could help you at home. When you're a mom one day, you'll understand what I mean in saying how comforting it is to know that your children are in a school system filled with caring teachers.

When I met with Mrs. Haselman, Mrs. Hazelton and Mr. Kincaid to discuss the goals of your IEP for second grade, your teachers were happy with all the progress you made this year. There are certain things we need to work on this summer that will help you in second grade. You need to improve in knowing the difference between short and long vowel sounds and how to count money correctly. Then your teachers each made a point to say how much they enjoyed having you and how much they would miss you. Mr. Kincaid laughed and said, "I loved kidding Avery. I enjoyed picking on her and she enjoyed picking on me right back!"

I cannot wait to see the exciting learning experiences that lie ahead for you in second grade!

Love you forever,
Mom

Innocence Unleashed

School was out. No little girl embraced this freedom more than Avery who scampered barefoot through the backyard in pursuit of the lightning bugs that blinked in the summer night. She squealed each time she caught one and yelled, "Mom, look! I caught another one. That makes five. They're tickling my hands! Mom, are you and Dad watching?"

Brad nodded from his lounge chair and Kim yelled, "We're watching, Avery. You're so good!"

"I know! I'm the best lightning bug catcher ever. What should I do with them? I better let them go. If I put them in a jar they might die, huh?"

"That's right. You need to let them go. It's your bedtime."

That wasn't the response that spunky Avery wanted to hear; so she ignored her mother and continued to run through the soft grass calling, "Come here, lightning bugs! I won't hurt you."

Finally needing to catch her breath from the chase, Avery plopped on the ground with clenched fists. She encouraged her cat, Buttercup, to sit on her lap. This was a welcome relief for her four-legged friend who was weary from trying to keep pace all night.

Burying her face in the whispery calico fur, Avery shared the plan with her confidante. "Let's pretend we don't hear Mom. I'm not ready for bed. Maybe she and Dad will keep talking for a while."

Then Brad hollered, "It's time for bed. Now!" With that, Avery opened her sweaty palms and freed the prisoners. "Look, Buttercup. They're blinking like crazy! Betcha they're happy I let 'em go."

Two seconds later, she came bounding towards the deck. Kim braced herself in the chair, knowing full well that the free spirit in red polka dot pajamas would vault onto her lap. Avery warned, "Here I come, Mom, ready or not!"

It was a perfect landing and Avery howled in laughter as she threw her arms around Kim's neck and cheered, "Hooray! Another perfect jump for me! I love playing this game, Mom. Don't you? I'm not ready for bed so what should we do now? I know! Let's go have a snack. Dad, you can come too."

Trying not to laugh aloud, Brad said, "We know what you're up to, young lady. You've already had your bedtime snack. Did you think we forgot?"

The full moon illuminated Avery's deep dimples as she deceptively giggled, "I was trying to trick you!"

Kim yawned after a busy day at work and somewhat firmly said, "Babe, I'm really tired and so is your dad. No more tricks. Go brush your teeth and I'll come tuck you in."

"Just tell me one adventure story first. Try to make it funny like Nena does. Her stories are better than yours."

"I know they are," Kim admitted. "When I was little, your Nena told me and my sisters lots of adventure stories. We loved them."

"Isn't it funny that my Nena is your mommy? You're lucky you have three sisters. I love Joy and Kari and Libby. They're so nice to me. I wish I had a sister. All I got was a brother and Tanner bosses me around all the time. That isn't fair, is it?"

"Avery Renee, you know Tanner is a good brother. You're just as guilty as he is when you argue. You both know how to push each other's buttons." Avery grinned in victory knowing how mad it made Tanner when she raced to the bathroom every night to brush her teeth first.

"Guess what I did one day in school this year when I saw Tanner? I ran over and gave him a big hug. He didn't even get mad."

Kim smiled. "See. I told you he was a good brother."

She and Brad looked at one another, knowing they needed to take Tanner aside later and compliment him for not getting upset when Avery's spontaneity had no doubt embarrassed him in front of his classmates.

Brad then picked up his light-weight fireball and said, "It's time to brush your teeth."

Despite warning Avery not to argue as he carried her into the house, she had the last word. "Just because Tanner is 10, it's unfair he gets to stay all night with the Tabler boys. Can I invite Hannah for a sleepover tomorrow night, Mom?"

"Avery, I'm too tired to argue. We'll see."

Brad returned 15 minutes later and reached for Kim's hand as he scooted his lounge chair close to hers. Though her eyes were closed, she wasn't startled by his gentle touch; the same chills raced through her as the night they first held hands as teenagers.

"The lightning bug girl is in bed. She just gave me orders that she's ready for you to tuck her in."

Kim couldn't ward off her smile. "I can't believe you got her in bed that quickly. How did that happen?"

Brad confessed with a mischievous grin. "I told her she could have Hannah stay over tomorrow night but only if it was okay with you."

"Did you promise her anything else?"

"Only that you'd help her catch lightning bugs," he laughed.

"It's no wonder she charms her way into getting things. She gets that from you, mister! Brad, I'm so proud of Tanner and how he handles things with Avery when he's with his friends. He's asked us different times what to say when she puts him on the spot with something she says or does."

"He gets it, Kim. We've told him to tell his friends she can't hear well and she's special. So that's what he does. He's protective of her in his own way. He always will be."

As Kim stood up so did Brad. He put his arms around his attractive wife's slender waist and whispered in her ear, "Two weeks from tonight is our wedding anniversary. That deserves a kiss." It was a sweet but short-lived moment as Avery bellowed, "Mom, where are you? Come tuck me in!"

Brad laughed. "I'll stay out here if you promise to be back within the hour. Good luck with that. She's wound up more than ever."

As Kim walked towards Avery's bedroom, she stopped short of entering and stepped back to hear the one-sided conversation she was having with her dolls that lined the bed.

"Okay, we're going to pretend we're in school until Mom gets here. I'm your first grade teacher and you are my students. You have to listen to me. Raise your hand if you have a question. My name is Mrs. Haselman and I'm going to teach you how to read better. You'll like me because I'm nice. If you need extra help with something you don't understand then Mrs. Hazelton will help you. She's nice too."

Kim covered her mouth to keep from laughing as the teacher continued to bark out directions to her obedient students. She had a perfect view of Avery's classroom that was decorated in vibrant hues of purple and the framed memory on the wall - the satin white dress Nena had made for that special day in church when Kim and Brad dedicated their lives to raising Avery in a loving environment and to introduce her to Christ at a young age.

"Okay, students, I'm tucking you all in," Avery said with authority. "I'm proud of you for being good listeners. Nighty night and sleep tight."

Never one to hide her emotions, Avery reprimanded Kim when she appeared. "Mom, where have you been? I kept yelling at you to tuck me in! Didn't you hear me?"

A gentle kiss on Avery's forehead erased her frustrations. "I heard you, sweetie. Dad and I were talking about you and Tanner and your final report cards for the school year. We're so proud of both of you."

"I did really good, didn't I? I tried really hard."

"You did a super job!"

"Mom, I was one of the smallest kids in first grade. Do you think I'll grow a whole bunch this summer?"

"You're growing, Avery, slowly but surely. Your dad and I aren't very tall either."

"I know but I bet you weren't as little as me when you were my age. I want to be like all the other kids. I'm the only one in my class who wears hearing aids. I wish I didn't have to wear them. Don't you?"

Kim fought back the tears that were gaining momentum. "Some kids have to wear glasses so they can see better. You need to wear hearing aids so you can hear better. They help you learn and talk more clearly. That's what matters, Avery. You know that, don't you? We've talked about this."

"Yeah, I know they help a lot but I still don't want kids to see them. I'm glad I have long hair to cover them up. What if somebody is mean and sees them and makes fun of me next year in school?"

"Ignore them. They aren't being mean on purpose. They just don't understand."

"I know, Mom, but if I start crying will you come get me?"

"Avery, I will always come get you. Don't ever worry about that. You have such wonderful teachers and friends who understand. Do you know what I'm saying?"

"Yeah. I know what you mean. I have the best friends in the world, especially Hannah. She sticks up for me if kids say I talk funny or talk too loud. She tells them it's because I have hearing aids. That's really nice of her, isn't it?"

"It's very nice. She's a sweet girl. Dad and I are thankful she's such a great friend."

"Yeah, she's my very best friend. I'm her very best friend too."

"Honey, we need to say our prayers now."

"I know. I'm getting sleepy. When we pray for me to be healthy tomorrow, can we pray for Buttercup to be healthy too?"

As she hugged her soft purple blanket, Kim gently laid her hand against Avery's cheek and prayed: *"Dear Lord, thank you for Avery. We ask that you will bless her with a good night's sleep and prepare the day that you have for her tomorrow. Help her to be a good friend to others and we ask that you will surround her with good friends as well. Lord, we pray health and protection over her. We also ask that you protect Buttercup. In Jesus' name we pray. Amen."*

"Mom, do you think Jesus heard you when you prayed for Buttercup?"

"Jesus always hears our prayers, sweetie."

"Great! Are you always going to tuck me in even when I get older? I like it when you put your hand on my cheek when we pray. It feels good."

"Babe, I'm going to tuck you in for as long as you let me."

"That's good because I can't go to sleep if you don't."

Kim wrapped her arms around her capricious daughter. "Your dad and I love you so much. Now you really need to close your eyes and go to sleep."

As Kim covered her up and kissed her soft cheek, Avery whispered, "Dad already helped me take out my hearing aids. He said Hannah can come for a sleepover tomorrow night."

"I know," Kim whispered back. "You can call Hannah tomorrow."

"I love you, Mommy. Nighty night and sleep tight."

"I love you, Avery. Nighty night and sleep tight."

"Wait! Before you turn out the light, tell me when Bible school starts. Is it in a few weeks?"

"It is. Are you looking forward to it?"

"Yeah. It's a lot of fun. If my teacher asks us where Jesus is, I'm going to raise my hand first. I'm going to say the same thing I said last year. Jesus is in my heart."

"That's the perfect answer. It makes my heart smile that you know this. I'm turning off the light now."

"Wait! I just have to tell you one more thing. I've been

thinking about what I want to be when I grow up. I want to be a cat doctor or a Mom. What did you want to be when you were my age?"

"Ever since I can remember, I've always wanted to be a Mom. It's the best job in the world."

"Do you make a lot of money?"

"You don't make any money but you get lots of hugs and kisses."

"Perfect! I can be a Mom and a cat doctor at the same time. I just love it when Buttercup purrs. It sounds so pretty. That's my favorite sound. What's your favorite sound?"

"Oh, that's easy! My favorite sound is when you and Tanner say you love me. No more questions, young lady. "

Brad was nearly asleep by the time Kim joined him on the deck. "She is such a chatterbox. As much as she wears me out some days, I think about those moments when we didn't know if she'd ever be able to talk."

There was no opportunity for Brad to respond because Avery barged onto the deck. "Are you guys talking about me?"

This time Brad did have a chance to respond. "We're not telling you again to get in bed. If you want to invite Hannah for a sleepover, you better get a move on it!"

"Wait! I just have one more thing to say. Mom always tells Jesus thank you for me when we pray. I want to say my own prayer tonight. So both of you have to close your eyes. I'm going to put my hands on your cheeks. Here it goes. *Thank you, Jesus, for Buttercup and Hannah and Tanner. Thank you for Mom and Dad who love me and listen to me. Amen and goodnight. I'm going to bed now.*"

Second Grade

*P*rior to the start of the school year, it was time for Avery to pick up her new hearing aids. She was looking forward to it.

"I really like the brown ones you picked out, sweetie. It's good that you went with a solid color instead of the giraffe print you also liked."

Avery looked confused. "Why, Mom?"

"Well, these need to last a couple of years. We can't buy new ones whenever we want to because they're very expensive. I thought you might get tired of the others but you won't with these."

"Will I have to wear hearing aids when I'm a teenager or a Mom?"

"You will, Avery. If they help you hear better, then don't you think the best thing is to wear them?"

She didn't answer so Kim repeated the question. There was still a long pause until she finally said, "Yeah, I do."

Kim shared the conversation with Brad that night. "She's asked me similar questions like that a lot more lately. She's naturally becoming more conscientious the older she gets. I'm hoping if we continue to make her realize how much better she hears with them, she'll be able to shake the ridicule that might be ahead in the next few years and not worry what others might say. I think I'll send her new teacher an email about this. I also need to mention that Avery might have a sore in her ear."

Monday, August 27, 2012 10:08 PM

Hello Mrs. Swihart.

I had a very talkative little girl today when I got home from work. She had a great first day of school and talked about it all night long. I tried to tell her at supper that she needed to stop talking and eat her supper while it was still warm. Then I reminded myself that her constant talking is actually an answer to prayers we said years ago when we realized she was hearing impaired. We wondered if she would ever talk normally. So I enjoyed listening to her all night long. When I asked her to put her binder in her backpack at 8 o'clock, she said, "Mom, do I really have to? I just want to keep looking at it." Thank you for making her first day so wonderful!

I didn't really get much of a chance to talk to you about Avery's hearing aids the night of the open house at school. I have asked her teachers in the past to please keep an eye out for her in the event that someone might say something mean or hurtful. When some kids have raised questions, the teachers have explained that she needs them to hear better like some kids need glasses to see better. I don't anticipate any problems. I know that the day will eventually come when she might be the subject of a joke and I'm dreading that so much.

She was complaining tonight of some ear pain. I think she may have a sore in the left ear and I'm going to check it in the morning before school. I may need to make an appointment to have it examined. I wanted to let you know in case I need to have an early dismissal for her on Tuesday or Wednesday.

Thank you for all your help.
Kim

Tuesday, August 28, 2012 7:42 AM

Thank you for your note, Kim. I'm so glad Avery had a good first day yesterday. This seems like a very nice class and I am looking forward to a good year with them.

Thanks for the heads up on the ear pain she has been experiencing and I will keep an eye out for this. I will also be sensitive about the comments that others make and hopefully Avery will continue to experience caring and acceptance from her peers. She is a lovely girl!

Sincerely,
Dawn Swihart

Kim had such a good feeling about the start of Avery's school year and with good reason. She had immediately developed a wonderful rapport with Mrs. Swihart and was further encouraged when she learned that Mrs. Hazelton would again be Avery's intervention specialist.

Friday, September 28, 2012 3:04 PM

Hi Kim,

With progress reports coming out today, I thought it would be a good time to touch base and see how you feel things are going this year. Are there any specific areas of concern where we can make changes? I know you have had some concerns with science and I have been working with Mrs. Swihart to increase Avery's level of success. Regarding spelling, she's had some success with the 10 words and 2 sentences so I'll plan on sticking with that for now.

In math, I have been working on general number sense skills (place value, tens and ones, work on a hundred's chart, greater than/less than, etc.) during small group intervention. She also comes by herself once a week to work on the coin counting. I feel that she's making gains. Of course, I need to consult with Mrs. Swihart to see if she's carrying over her skills from my room to the regular classroom. Avery's oral reading is coming along with the majority of her errors revolving around vowel patterns; we'll just have to keep working at it! Please let me know if you have any concerns at this time and throughout the year.

Thanks and have a nice weekend!
Sara Hazelton

Avery enjoyed second grade immensely, especially when Mrs. Swihart let the students be involved with hands-on learning experiments during science class. She described some of them to Kim when she was getting ready for school.

"I'm going to miss the experiments, Mom. They were a lot of fun but I'm still glad it's only two more weeks until school is out."

As Kim combed her hair, she said, "You've done another great job this year. Dad and I are always proud of how hard you work."

"I did work hard! It seems like I have to learn a lot more each year. I need a break."

"It's going to be so hot today, sweetie. How about letting me put your hair in a ponytail?"

Avery's response was quick and adamant. "No! I don't want kids to see my hearing aids. They might make fun of me. I'll wear a ponytail this summer but not to school."

Kim fought back the tears. "That's fine. Let me put this barrette in your hair and you can go outside on the porch and wait for the bus. Tanner will be right there."

As soon as Avery was out the door, Kim began to cry. She tried to hide the sound of her intermittent sobbing. "Tanner, the bus will be here any minute."

She retreated to the kitchen in the hopes that he wouldn't see her. What she didn't realize is that he had heard everything, including her conversation with Avery. When Kim turned around and saw him standing there, she apologized immediately. "Tanner, I'm so sorry you have to see me like this. It just breaks my heart that Avery worries about kids making fun of her."

"I know. I feel sorry for Avery too."

Then he did what he had seen his dad do when she was crying like this. Tanner gave his mom a hug.

Kim made a point to be standing in the driveway when they got off the bus. There were no visible remains of her emotional morning. "Hey, I hope you both had a great day! How did school go?"

Tanner didn't have time to answer because he was in a hurry to grab his bat and glove and play baseball with the Tabler boys. Avery, on the other hand, had a lot to share.

"Mom, I have a surprise for you and Dad! Want me to get it out of my binder and show you? You're going to be so happy! I wrote you something. Mrs. Swihart helped me but I did most of the work. Do you want to read it?"

"I want you to read it to me. How about that?"

"Yeah, that would be good. I'll read it to you now and then I'll read it to Dad when he gets home from work."

"That would be perfect."

"Okay, I'm going to start reading now."

Dear Mom and Dad,

In second grade I learned how to write in cursive. I am proud that I can do cursive writing. I am proud of me that I can read good. I hope I can do better in math next year. I was surprised when I got Bulldog of the Month. I hope you are proud of me too!

Love,
Avery

"Do you like it, Mom?"

Kim put both arms around her and kissed her forehead. "I love it! You're amazing!"

"Why are there tears in your eyes if you love it?"

"These are happy tears, sweetie."

"Yeah, I know what you mean. I had happy tears when Buttercup had her baby kittens."

On the last day of school, Kim was standing in the driveway

to greet Tanner and Avery once again when they got off the bus. Avery raced to hug her. "Mom, I passed second grade! Mrs. Swihart said some really nice things about me on my report card. There are some big words I don't know so you need to help me."

They read the good news together: 'Avery needs to practice add/subtract facts and needs to take more time when writing to produce neat work on daily assignments. She does well following school rules. Keep forth your good effort to complete your work, Avery. You have been a pleasure to have in class this year.'

From the Heart

Dear Tanner and Avery,

We're going as a family to the Putnam County Relay for Life tonight. I was in my first one in 2001 when I was pregnant with you, Tanner. I've told you that I had cancer when I was a teenager but you're both too young to understand just how serious my disease was and how sick I got from the treatments. I couldn't have gotten through it all without the support and strength of your dad, my family members and my friends. By God's grace, I have been a cancer survivor for 18 years.

This event we attend every June is to raise money for cancer research. It's important for you to know why I cherish being part of it. Every year, I look for my walking partner, Earl Goodwin. He is my Aunt Pam's dad. He is also a cancer survivor and we have walked every relay together. Each year, Earl makes sure to remind me that I don't have to walk at the slower pace his body requires and that I can go ahead of him. And every year I say, "There is no way I'm leaving you." In recent years, Aunt Pam and Earl's wife, Elsie, have joined our survivor walking group.

You know that the tradition is for the survivors to begin the event by walking one lap together on a track that is lined with family members, friends and supporters. The loud clapping and roaring cheers for all of us are unforgettable. I get emotional every year when I see your dad and my family rooting me on in celebration of my life. You don't remember any of this but there were years when I pushed you in a stroller or you walked around the track holding my hand.

Let me share with you the loving sentiments that my sisters sent me recently. They reflect God's love and our family's love for each other.

Dear Kim,

I don't recall the exact time when Mom and Dad told us about your cancer. I do remember praying for you a lot. I also remember your lying in the hospital bed in Toledo and being so sick. I'll never forget the night your hair started falling out and seeing Mom's reaction and yours. That's when it really hit me how seriously ill you were; tears well inside me as I recall this.

Kari and Libby and I were so young and had never been around anyone with cancer. We didn't know what to expect. Even though we watched you suffer, Mom and Dad tried so hard to shield us. I will always remember watching you play volleyball and running track with your ball cap on. You were so inspirational.

I have tremendous respect for you, Kim. I now deal with cancer patients on a daily basis with my job. Because of you, I have so much sympathy and compassion for them. I can't imagine how hard it was for you and our parents. I'll never forget that saying: 'Tough times never last; tough people do.' This has been a strong reference I've leaned on many times in my life.

Love,
Joy

Dear Kim,

Even though I was too young to understand the severity of what you were going through, I vividly remember the day that Mom and Dad took us to see you in the hospital. Your white blood cell count had dropped so low that they thought you might not make it.

The thing that sticks in my mind visually and emotionally is when I was sitting at the kitchen bar with Mom and talking about school. I remember this being a very special time for me because I was getting one-on-one time with Mom. You got out of the shower and walked into the kitchen with a towel wrapped around you. Mom knew by the look on your face that something was seriously wrong and she followed you into the bathroom. This was the first time your hair had started to fall out. You and Mom were crying. I remember feeling confused at such a young age. Now I am ashamed to say that I felt a little jealous of the attention I was getting from Mom until she walked away to be with you.

I admire your strength and determination as you endured this battle, Kim. I also admire how you live your life now and share your testimony. You have turned that negative experience into a positive one. I believe that's wholly from God. Our family's firm foundation never wavered, even though Satan threw his best at us.

Love,
Kari

Dear Kim,

I was only six years old when you were diagnosed with cancer so this was scary stuff. The memory that really lingers for me is the day I was home from school sick with the flu. You were sick, too, only it was from your chemotherapy treatments. We spent the day together lying in Mom and Dad's bed and watching TV. I can still hear the haunting tone in your voice when you told me that you would rather die than go through the cancer. I didn't know what to say.

You have truly been a testament of a cancer survivor. You are so strong and you never gave up the fight. Now when the conversation comes up with my friends that you had cancer, they are in such shock and question how we all ever got through this. My response is always the same. Even though I was too young to remember the details, our family got through it with God's help and our faith. The Relay for Life event is always an emotional time for all of us because it is a celebration of the road that God has placed before you and Brad.

Love,
Libby

Even though so many years have passed since I had cancer, I know that life is short and that we need to count our blessings daily. We can be here today and gone tomorrow. I want my life to be a thankful reminder of this to each of you. I want you to feel compassion when you see someone who is bald from chemotherapy treatments and say to yourself, "You can get through this. Our mom did." If you meet someone with any type of impairment or physical struggle, you need to offer encouragement. It will mean more to them than you will ever know.

You were both chosen by your teachers as the 'Bulldog of the Month' at the same time this year. The theme was 'self-esteem.' Do you remember when you asked me what self-esteem is? I said it was like the armor you carry with you to face the challenges that come your way. Your teachers chose you because they see the confidence you have in yourselves and the positive attitudes you show in class and to your classmates. I'm so proud of both of you!

Your dad and I enjoy watching every softball game you're playing, Avery. You've improved so much. You've been able to hit the pitch nearly every time. And Tanner, your baseball season is going so well. Even though you make me sit on the edge of my seat each time you try to steal the bases, I absolutely love cheering you on. As I write this, your Aunt Libby is about to get married. She is carrying on the tradition of being married in an outdoor ceremony at Nena and Papa's house, just like the rest of their daughters have. You are both so excited to be in the wedding.

My parents instilled in me how important it is to have a personal relationship with Christ. I hope that your dad and I are doing the same for each of you. I could not be the wife, mother, sister or friend to others that I am today without leaning on Him daily for guidance. Yes, I struggle from time to time and fail. There have been so many times in my life when I thought I could handle things by myself. There have also been times when I thought my way of doing things was better than God's way.

I admit that it is hard to trust His ways when they don't always make sense to me but I need to always remember that God is on my side. He is in my corner and is fighting for me. He'll always be there for you too. I pray in the years ahead that you will form a close relationship with Christ and learn like I have that God is always there to 'listen to me.'

Love you forever,
Mom

About the Author

Beth Huffman, a retired English teacher, is a professional inspirational speaker and author from Columbus Grove, Ohio. 'Listen to Me' is her third book. Her other books are 'Run, Amy, Run!' and 'Awesome Andrea' that depict the lives of courageous heroes born with cystic fibrosis. Profits from these two books go to the Cystic Fibrosis Foundation for research.

To learn more about Beth's mission as an author and speaker, please go to her website at: www.danceintherain.me or contact her at: bethhm@roadrunner.com

NEED ADDITIONAL COPIES?

To order more copies of

Listen to Me

contact NewBookPublishing.com

❏ Order online at:
NewBookPublishing.com/ListentoMe

❏ Call 877-311-5100 or

❏ Email Info@NewBookPublishing.com